MW01068680

In praise of
Homeodynamic Recovery Method

I just wanted to let you know that we had a mini group session with the dietician today. She was speaking about how we work with a meal plan and then she went on to specifically recommend the ED Institute website and the HDRM. I almost jumped out of my seat!! I was so excited to hear her endorse the ED Institute to the group. She told everyone how the meal plan is just a minimum, how people on HDRM had eaten to hunger cues and done so well on it, she talked about set point theory - she was so much behind everything on the Eating Disorder Institute website.

– Zoe

I just started a day program for anorexia treatment/weight restoration this week. Your blog post about what to expect during the phases of recovery answered all of my questions, concerns, misapprehensions and silly-but-insomnia-causing irrational fears better than anyone at this clinic so far - and it's a freaking well-run clinic, haha. Thank you. Thank you so so much for the detail, clinical and psychological insight and fact, and COMPASSION that you put into this website, and that post.

– Bridget

I just want to say thank you so much for this website. It has been a life saver, literally, for me and my daughter. She was dismissed by the doctor as not quite skinny enough to qualify for help, and I was dismissed as too controlling. I have felt desperate, but the information and support that you provide on this site has been so so good, and helpful. All the facts about what to expect in recovery, what is normal, and the barriers she has to get through have genuinely been her constant companion and guide. Thank you.

– Rachel

Doctors said without drastic changes, I would have 2 to 3 weeks left to live, as all my organs were beginning to shut down after almost 6 years of Anorexia. I was so sick that I thought that maybe it would be the best for me and anybody else if I could just disappear. Doctors gave me until the next day to think about everything and tell them how and if I wanted to continue treatment. The night after that appointment, I remembered that somebody once mentioned something about the HDRM guidelines and without really expecting a lot, I took a look at your blog. In this night, I read about three quarters of your blog posts, watched all your videos, read recovery stories from people in remission and did a ton of research on my own. And I cannot really say that it was an "Aha"-moment. I don't know exactly how it happened, but when I went to bed in the early morning, I had new hope, new determination and new motivation. What's strange is that the guidelines are actually not different from what my care team was telling me: "Eat, rest and cognitive behavioral therapy". But something about the way you explain things, how you write and talk just broke down all the walls I had built around me. After talking everything through very carefully with my care team the next day, I started my own personal HDRM-journey.

– *Julia*

I just came across your incredible site and I HAD TO EXPRESS MY APPRECIATION. I am a licensed clinical psychologist specializing in the treatment of ED and am beyond grateful for the tireless work and effort you have put into creating the ED Institute. I look forward to sharing this resource with patients and colleagues. Thank you for creating such an influential resource. Words can't express my appreciation and gratitude.

– *Janelle*

The Eating Disorder Institute

www.edinstitute.org

The mission of The Eating Disorder Institute is to help patients become *"the expert in the room".*

Patient advocacy is a practice wherein the focus is on empowering patients. Health care provision these days renders both patient and practitioner progressively more responsible for having the health care delivery system run smoothly rather than realize the best outcomes for the patient.

In an excessively fattist and healthist society (wherein we discriminate against and stigmatize those with fatness and/or illness), the opportunity to receive adequate care and support when one has an active eating disorder is poor. Not only are there inadequate services to begin with, but the majority with the condition is excluded from adequate care exclusively on the unscientific premise that body mass reflects health status.

The Eating Disorder Institute provides scientific data for the purpose of having it applied in real-life circumstances, with presumed explicit support and advice from qualified health care providers, either to mitigate quality and length of life impacts and/or to navigate this chronic condition into a state of full remission.

Other books by Gwyneth Olwyn

Journal (vols 1..6 in 6 different colours)

ISBN 978-1475001730

A personal journal to support those recovering from eating disorders. The journal contains both a food log and diary-style pages as well as excerpts related to recovery from the edinstitute.org website.

RECOVER
FROM
EATING DISORDERS

RECOVER FROM EATING DISORDERS

The Homeodynamic Recovery Method

GWYNETH OLWYN

EATING DISORDER INSTITUTE

Akureyri Publishing

Vancouver

Printed in USA

Olwyn, Gwyneth.

Recover from eating disorders: the homeodynamic recovery method / Gwyneth Olwyn. – 1st ed.

  p.   cm.

Includes bibliographical references and index.

ISBN-13: 978-1500828257

ISBN: 1500828254

Akureyri Publishing ISBN 978-1-500-82825-7

First published in Canada by Akureyri Publishing

First Edition: July 2017

10 9 8 7 6 5 4 3 2 1

For all those who live with eating disorders.

"Acceptance doesn't mean resignation. It means
understanding that something is what it is and
there's got to be a way through it."

Michael J. Fox

Acknowledgments

It was my intention to publish this guide many years ago. And while I fully expect that in a few more years I will look back on this guide and want to further edit and update it, you eventually have to put a bow on things and hope that it is sufficiently comprehensive and useful to your readership.

All possible errors, oversights and mistakes in this guide are mine and mine alone. I was fortunate enough to have two professional book and research editors review the drafts of this guide and offer me invaluable feedback. Thank you Kerrie Baldwin and Ruth Leach for your ability to call out when I lost my train of thought and for giving me some absolutely brilliant reordering of paragraphs that made the hopelessly unclear suddenly make absolute sense. That you gifted me with your professional editing of the guide is a debt I cannot repay.

To Andrea LaMarre, Tetyana Pekar and Elizabeth Watson my thanks for your razor-sharp brains, wit and for inherently refusing to settle.

Lynh, Nicola, Heidi, Pauline and Heather who have shared their personal experiences of recovery, you are all so very dear to my heart. The challenges and successes that you have relayed to me over the years have become the soul of the entire Eating Disorder Institute. Without your input, I would truly have no understanding of eating disorders because all the peer-reviewed published material in the world is useless if it cannot be translated into any kind of lived outcome.

There are too many ED Institute community members to name, but each one of you has had a hand in making what is the best of this guide a reality.

To the three Rachels, you know who you are, it is humbling for me on a daily basis that you taught me more than I could ever possibly offer to each of you. Rare is the day that you are all not on my mind.

To Greg, you already know. To Tim and Scott, your faith in me gets me through. To my entire sprawling family, I love you guys. And to Jon Snow (who knows nothing) the cat who quite literally hung on my every word as I typed, given his preferred space is draped over my arm (I have the elbow callous to prove it).

Gwyneth Olwyn, Vancouver, July 2017

Contents

Seek medical advice

This guide is not a replacement for qualified, in-person medical or psychological advice. If you are attempting to recover from an eating disorder, do not apply the Homeodynamic Recovery Method without seeking qualified medical input.

Nothing within this guide can be interpreted as medical advice.

Author's Note

The Homeodynamic Recovery Method (HDRM, formerly the MinnieMaud™ method) was developed to help adults with eating disorders navigate the process of recovery to achieve remission. Originally outlined on the Eating Disorder Institute website, the Homeodynamic Recovery Method is now synthesized and outlined in this step-by step guide. It is my hope that this guide will also make it easier for patients to discuss the Homeodynamic Recovery Method with their health care providers and families.

Some topics that pertain to recovery may not be covered in sufficient depth in this guide, and on those occasions I will reference specific papers and posts that can be found on www.edinstitute.org.

Please note that while I use female pronouns throughout this guide, the prevalence of eating disorders is not gender-based. As such, please infer an absolutely gender-neutral position despite the implication that it is somehow a female-only condition.

I also use the term "fat" in this guide and I use it in connection to its role as a metabolic modulator within our bodies and not as a term of derision or criticism. I will also use the term "obesity" and that will be only in the context of referencing research.

Introduction

"Lynnard," a community member on the forums of the Eating Disorder Institute was encouraged by other members to share with me the following excerpt from the *Velveteen Rabbit*.

"Real isn't how you are made," said the Skin Horse. "It's a thing that happens to you. When a child loves you for a long, long time, not just to play with, but REALLY loves you, then you become Real."

"Does it hurt?" asked the Rabbit.

"Sometimes," said the Skin Horse, for he was always truthful. "When you are Real you don't mind being hurt."

"Does it happen all at once, like being wound up," he asked, "or bit by bit?"

"It doesn't happen all at once," said the Skin Horse. "You become. It takes a long time. That's why it doesn't often happen to people who break easily, or have sharp edges, or who have to be carefully kept. Generally, by the time you are Real, most of your hair has been loved off, your eyes drop out and you get loose joints and very shabby. But these things don't matter at all, because once you are Real you can't be ugly, except to people who don't understand." [1]

The Skin Horse speaks of Realness in a way that likely resonates for all of us, but the quote is particularly meaningful for those who pursue remission from an eating disorder.

Not everyone who achieves remission from an eating disorder experiences, or even needs to experience, a transformation to Realness. But often, traveling through the maze toward remisseion does make you Real—able to be okay with being hurt, and okay with understanding that you can't be ugly except to those who don't understand.

And of course the rabbit, within the context of its prominent appearance in the Homeodynamic Recovery Method logo, represents an invitation to explore the truth all while coming to terms with its elusive nature—just as Alice follows the white rabbit in *Alice's Adventures in Wonderland*. For most adults with eating disorders, remission has several odds stacked against it. Our approach to eating today is steeped in fear mongering and moralizing to such a degree that those with eating disorders get no respite from the unrelenting anxiety that any given food choice or activity might be wrong. Therefore, remission is found underground: down the rabbit hole.

There are no evidence-based treatment options for adults with eating disorders. Additionally, there is no cure for anyone who has an eating disorder. The condition can be moved into remission, which gives the person the same quality and length of life that would be expected for someone who had never had an eating disorder. However, remission is harder to realize for adults and there are likely several reasons for that fact:

1. Cultural factors today make communal eating less likely for adults than for children or adolescents. Communal eating is one of several important facets for getting to remission, as it helps someone with an eating disorder practice approaching and eating food (explained fully in chapter 2).

2. The poor rates of remission for adults: only 20% success for those who have had the condition for 5-10 years, and only 10% success where the condition has been present beyond 10 years.[2] The lackluster remission rate creates a circular disinterest for investing in adult treatment because the outcomes are so poor. Obviously, the lack of treatment assures that outcomes cannot improve.

3. The outcomes for early intervention with children and adolescents are sufficiently impressive (within the first year of onset, up to 90% will reach remission[3] with appropriate treatment), it is understandable, but not acceptable, that both research and treatment funding remains focused on early intervention.

Recover from Eating Disorders: Homeodynamic Recovery Method Step by Step Guide has been developed for adults with eating disorders to provide much needed information on how to achieve remission. Certainly, there are no guarantees when it comes to your journey through recovery, but it can be much less intimidating if you are given a compass, a map and some sense of what markers you should look for as you navigate recovery—and that is what this guide sets out to do. The Homeodynamic Recovery Method is an analysis and synthesis of scientific research that demonstrates how remission is achieved for adults with eating disorders. Far better than 10-20% success rates can be achieved when adequate treatment is provided to adult populations.

Predominantly patients who have applied the Homeodynamic Recovery Method for reaching remission from an eating disorder are adults between the ages of 22-55, with outliers who are both younger and older as well. Most are living, studying and working in community settings, although several patients in hospital settings have applied this method with their treatment team's support and guidance as well. The vast majority has a history of active eating disorder behavior and a significant number were once hospitalized, or receiving some type of formal medical care for the condition, directly as a result of the eating disorder's impact on their health. Some stumbled upon the information on the Eating Disorder Institute website having had no prior insight that the various health problems they faced had the common underlying cause of an eating disorder. For these individuals, some had an acute eating disorder in their teen years and believed they had been cured through the treatment they received at that time. Instead, they were mired in maintaining a goal weight that had been assigned to them by the treatment team involved, and as a result had maintained an ongoing sub-clinical eating disorder that continued to erode their health and quality of life. Still others were surprised to learn their insomnia, coldness, gastrointestinal problems, food intolerances, headaches and infertility might all be attributable to what they believed, and many health care providers directly reinforce with them, were acceptable healthy eating and exercising behaviors.

Because our society currently reveres restrictive eating and rigorous exercising as demonstrable signs of health, it is a growing problem that many with active eating disorders are mired in being treated for symptoms of an eating disorder rather than receiving treatment for the eating disorder itself.

Before I venture into how this guide is set out, there are two additional things you need to know about me, the author. Firstly, I have no history of an eating disorder. This fact is relevant to you because between half to three-quarters of those working in the field of eating disorders have personal histories of the condition (for either themselves, or a family member). Secondly, I am a patient advocate and have no affiliations with any organization, association or corporate interest that might conflict with my ability to provide as much information as possible to help you become an informed and empowered patient.

Patient advocates don't diagnose or treat ailments at all. Their work resides in a lay specialty area surrounding various facets of the health care industry. Most people have no idea what patient advocates do because the field is fairly new, and practitioners work in very distinct and seemingly unrelated areas such as the legal profession, ombudsmen within hospital settings, and private practitioners in various specialties (e.g. geriatric, palliative, critical, or chronic illness care).

Step by step

Recover from Eating Disorders: Homeodynamic Recovery Method Step by Step Guide can be read cover to cover or out of sequence by chapter and also serves as a quick reference as you move through recovery.

Additionally, if you decide to apply another science-based method for reaching remission, this guide will remain useful to you. Much of the information on the symptoms in recovery and risks associated with re-feeding are relevant no matter the method of recovery you choose to apply.

Chapter 1 provides some important background within the context of how the medical and psychiatric communities define and treat the condition. Beyond the terminology, statistics and prognosis, the confusion surrounding its definition as a mental illness is reviewed within the context of how to apply the Homeodynamic Recovery Method. Chapter 2 outlines how best to determine if you, or someone you love, has an eating disorder and it explains how the eating disorder is experienced by the patient, both subjectively and (as best as we understand it today) objectively within the mind and body. Chapter 3 delves into all the science that shapes the Homeodynamic Recovery Method. Chapter 4 lays out in detail the Homeodynamic Recovery Method and its three-legged stool for reaching remission: re-feeding, resting and (brain) re-training. Additionally, chapter 4 describes common medical risks, common misdiagnoses, energy intake guidelines, extreme hunger, phases of recovery, and the nature of pain in recovery.

Chapter 5 looks at how best to identify key health care practitioners who might be able to help you reach your goal of remission. The chapter also looks at the relevant psychoeducational treatment options, and the drug treatment options that are, and are not, available. Additionally this chapter explains how to interpret scientific data. Chapter 6 reviews all the challenges associated with pursuing remission in relation to your real world experiences with work, school, family, friends, and colleagues. Examples, techniques, and exercises are included in this chapter to help you learn how to protect your recovery efforts.

Chapter 7 looks at how remission is defined, common causes of relapse, and how to develop a relapse reversal intervention kit to ensure your remission remains intact indefinitely.

Recover, but not too much

As a patient advocate I have worked exclusively with patients managing eating disorders for the past nine years. While the step by step in depth information in this guide will benefit any adult with an eating disorder looking to improve her quality of life or to reach remission; I believe that the minority dissent I bring to treatment options for adults has even greater value in increasing the chance that a patient will reach full remission. Minority dissent is commonly the only thing that squelches the absolutely catastrophic outcomes that can occur with groupthink.[4] The groupthink that currently plagues treatment programs for adults with eating disorders today is the idea that restoring an energy deficit in the body is achieved through restoring weight to a body mass index that is natural for only 4% of our population.

The guidelines of the Homeodynamic Recovery Method comprise nothing that is not found in any science-based inpatient or residential treatment program out there today, with one glaring exception: the Homeodynamic Recovery Method rejects the current culturally derived and unscientific approach that a patient must recover, but not too much. Recovering not too much manifests as returning to various restrictive and compensatory behaviors at a sub-clinical level as a way to maintain a target weight.

The excessive food intake necessary in recovery is not a harbinger for the development of binge eating or bulimia.[5] No scientific evidence supports that widespread attitude. In fact, it is the fundamental misunderstanding of energy management within the human system that dooms most patients to a slow and inexorable decline toward severely impaired quality of life and health.

A patient does not develop bulimia or binge-eating behaviors unless she persists with constant attempts to under-eat in response to energy demands that far exceed her desired intake levels.[6] It's not the eating that's the problem; it's the restriction. One of the most fascinating aspects of human nature is that we can readily see the failures strewn across medical history, yet we are unshakeable in our faith that we no longer suffer such similar errors in judgment today. If you have no interest in considering the possibility that common sense is often nonsensical, then this guide will likely be of no use to you. But if curiosity is nudging you forward, then please read on.

Why pursue remission?

As mentioned above, an eating disorder has no cure. Like almost all chronic conditions, it can be maneuvered into remission, but it can flare when and if circumstances trigger its reappearance. While I often use the term "recovery effort," no one has in fact "recovered" when they have successfully achieved full remission from an eating disorder.

Remission from any chronic condition has biomarkers that are indistinguishable from having never had the condition in the first place, but the condition is not gone; it is latent or hiding. It's tough enough to receive a diagnosis for any chronic condition, but tougher still is the fact that the patient doesn't get to go back to pre-condition status.

However, full remission from an eating disorder is maintained with fairly unobtrusive changes in lifestyle and the benefit is a quality and length of life that will mimic the experience of those who have never had an eating disorder in their lives.

Remission vs. harm reduction

Complete remission is an attainable state no matter the length of time or severity experienced by the patient. That is both a true and false statement. It is true in the sense that patients with an extremely severe and decades-long eating disorder will remit as readily as will patients with mild and short-lived symptoms of the same condition. It is false in that each patient lives within an entire multivariate system of environmental, sociocultural, familial, economic, psychological, biological, and genetic influences. It means that, independent of severity or length of time, the attainable nature of remission will vary with each patient's individual reality and circumstances.

And to complicate the matter further, that multivariate system is changing constantly. Therefore to view a state of remission as permanent and hierarchically superior to ongoing efforts at harm reduction is a complete failure to understand the fluidity of chronic conditions experienced over a lifetime.

If members of your treatment team have told you that you're not capable of reaching remission and you should focus your efforts on reducing the progressive harm associated with severe and enduring restrictive behaviors, realize that they can no more predict the arc of your living multivariate system any more than they could predict the weather in a year's time.

The Homeodynamic Recovery Method has been developed for patients who intend to pursue full remission from an eating disorder. The method can be applied at any time, at any age, and with any level of symptom severity, though never without adequate medical oversight of course.

If there is one undeniable truism when addressing a chronic condition in one's life, it's that the maxim "know thyself" takes on heightened importance.

Whether the journey of attempting remission leads you to recognize that yours is ultimately a path that will include remission or not, always hold the juxtaposition of both realities (remission and harm reduction) in your mind at once. In that way you will always maximize your quality and length of life. But more importantly, you will know yourself at a level that will make your life more meaningful, precious, and fulfilling, no matter how an eating disorder might shape your path.

No assured outcomes

If anyone assures you that you will be cured, enter remission, or achieve any measurable outcome with eating disorder treatment, then reject those assurances outright. There are no assured outcomes.

To attempt to reach remission is not without its own inherent risk. Hindsight can make us regret taking a risk as equally as it can force us to regret having never taken a chance.

You will see dozens of recommendations on the Eating Disorder Institute site from patients who have reached complete remission applying the Homeodynamic Recovery Method and some will be found scattered throughout this guide as well. Those accounts are all genuine and deeply moving.

However, my job as a patient advocate is never to convert a patient. My job is to train a patient to become his or her own best advocate—to be the expert in the room. To become the best you can be at representing your own health interests, just remember there are no assured outcomes in life or in health status either.

Therefore I encourage you to read the rest of this guide with a critical and curious mind—exactly as one should approach following a white rabbit anywhere.

Endnotes for Introduction

1. Margery Williams, *The Velveteen Rabbit* (New York: Doubleday, 1992 & 1991), 5-9.

2. Olwyn, Gwyneth. "Part V UCSD EDC2014 Review." *The Eating Disorder Institute* (paper), January 31, 2015, https://www.edinstitute.org/conference/2015/1/31/part-v-ucsd-edc2014-review.

3. Ibid.

4. De Dreu, Carsten KW, and Michael A. West. "Minority dissent and team innovation: the importance of participation in decision making." *Journal of Applied Psychology* 86, no. 6 (2001): 1191.

5. Olwyn, Gwyneth. "Part II: What does BED really look like?" *The Eating Disorder Institute* (paper), July 10, 2015, https://www.edinstitute.org/paper/2015/7/10/part-ii-what-does-bed-really-look-like.

6. Olwyn, Gwyneth. "Binges Are Not Binges" *The Eating Disorder Institute* (paper), October 10, 2012, https://www.edinstitute.org/blog/2012/10/31/bingeing-is-not-bingeing.

Chapter One

Eating Disorders

Gwyneth: What do you wish you had known about the recovery process before you began?

Patient H: I wish I had known that recovery is not a straight path, and that anything can happen. I had recovered before as a teenager, and my recovery was pretty straightforward. My second go with recovery has been as different as night and day. I've had more recovery symptoms this time, and it was harder to let go of disordered thoughts and behaviors. It is incredibly important to have a therapist and/or supportive people in your recovery. Trying to recover on one's own is very difficult, and even though you can find supportive people in online environments, they can't take the place of a person willing to give you a hug if you need it, an ear to listen, and to encourage you each day.

Eating Disorders

What follows are a number of the mainstream technicalities that need introduction in order for you, as a patient, to be able to communicate with health care practitioners dedicated to diagnosing and treating eating disorders.

Definition

An eating disorder is best described as a chronic condition resulting from the misidentification of food as a threat; and as such it is best situated under the much larger umbrella of anxiety disorders. I will discuss this definition further in chapter 2. An eating disorder is currently defined as a mental illness within the Diagnostic and Statistical Manual of Mental Disorders (DSM) and psychiatrists are the only health care professionals tasked with submitting the clinical diagnosis that will be accepted by either private or national health insurance providers.

Classification

The DSM-5 divides eating disorders into three main classifications: anorexia nervosa (AN), bulimia nervosa (BN), and binge eating disorder (BED). This latest DSM edition has also added pica, rumination, and avoidant/restrictive food intake disorder (ARFID).

Additionally, there are these classifications: Other Specified Feeding and Eating Disorder (OSFED) and Unspecified Feeding and Eating Disorder (UFED), which ostensibly replace what was called Eating Disorder Not Otherwise Specified (EDNOS) as found in the DSM-IV.

Binge eating disorder (BED) was not identified as a stand-alone eating disorder by expert researchers[1] in the field and it was identified as a condition needing further study within the DSM-IV. BED in the DSM-5 has no connection to its definition within the DSM-IV. Those with BED, prior to the 2013 release of the DSM-5, were diagnosed with EDNOS.

The current definition of BED within the DSM-5 reflects cycles of restriction and reactive eating behaviors that do not rise to the severity listed for a diagnosis of BN. For more details and thorough references explaining BED within the DSM-5, please refer to the Eating Disorder Institute website papers on the topic.[2,3]

The inclusion of BED in the DSM-5 was contentious and involved concerning conflicts of interest.[4,5,6]

Out of the 18 panels tasked with developing recommendations for DSM-IV classifications, six had more than 80% of their members tied financially to the pharmaceutical industry. The eating disorder panel was one of those six, with 83% of its members tied to pharmaceutical industry support.[7] The number of panelists tied to pharmaceutical industries rose 14% overall from development of the DSM-IV to DSM-5.[8]

There was a push from independent researchers in the field of eating disorders to move towards a transdiagnostic approach by merging the five distinct classifications of eating disorders from the DSM-IV into one broad classification of eating disorder in the DSM-5. Transdiagnosis would have accurately reflected the clinical evidence that anorexia and bulimia are not two distinct conditions, and that several other eating and compensatory behaviors are all part of the same neurobiological condition as well.[9,10,11] This appropriate merger of classifications did not occur perhaps because too many special interests groups were involved in the development of the DSM-5.

I have no use for the DSM as not only is its provenance highly suspect, given pharmaceutical industry ties, but also it fails to reflect much of the recent genetic and neural research data that renders

DSM symptom checklists overly simplistic, subjective, and often inapplicable. Nonetheless, patients struggling to receive a diagnosis that will allow for financial coverage of their treatment must familiarize themselves with the DSM because its classifications are the only ones recognized by most national and private medical insurance organizations in the world's developed nations.

The International Classification of Diseases and Related Health Problems (ICD-10) is sometimes used in place of the DSM for diagnosis; however the classifications found within both tomes are essentially interchangeable.

Symptomatology

Dr. Christopher Fairburn, a professor of psychiatry at Oxford University and a leader in the field eating disorder research and treatment, explains the symptoms associated with the eating disorder spectrum as follows:

... extreme dietary restraint and restriction, binge eating, self-induced vomiting and the misuse of laxatives, driven exercising, body checking and avoidance, and the over-evaluation of control over eating, shape and weight.[12]

Transdiagnosis recognizes the fact that those with an eating disorder can shift from one symptom to another or express several symptoms at the same time.

The terminology I find more useful and accurate in describing eating disorder symptoms is as follows:

- eating avoidance

- avoiding food intake and experiencing reactive eating sessions* in response to that restriction

- abuse of laxatives, diuretics, and purging to try to redress a reactive eating session

- using exercise to alleviate anxiety associated with eating or validating eating through "burning off" food intake

- abuse of prescription or illicit substances as a means to avoid food intake or reduce food absorption within the body

- applying rigid adherence to eating "healthily" or "cleanly" to alleviate anxiety associated with eating.

Causes

An eating disorder is an inherited neurobiological condition.

The genetic markers are not fully identified, but the condition usually lies dormant and may be triggered by innumerable environmental factors. The genetic predisposition for the condition is present in all human populations and even exists in some animals.[13,14] It has persisted within the human gene pool because it likely has, or once had, beneficial implications for survival.

---

* "Binge eating" is an inappropriate term for those with an eating disorder, for whom such eating sessions never occur in the absence of overall energy deficit within the body.

All manner of fancy research has been investigating the tantalizing suggestion that the dopaminergic reward systems in the brains of those with eating disorders are different than those of healthy controls.[15,16]

There is also plenty of fascinating stuff on the brain structures that may or may not be involved in miscasting food as the enemy. However, there are far more comprehensive sites and books on these topics than this guide. I will provide a layperson's view of the cascade from the moment an eating disorder is activated.

While the environmental factors that might activate an eating disorder in someone with the genetic predisposition can be anything from simply starting a diet, to undergoing surgery, catching a stomach bug, experiencing traumatic life events, to any situation you might care to name, none of those factors *causes* the condition; however they all have the capacity to generate energy deficits in the body, and in so doing they may activate the condition.

In other words, you won't get an eating disorder because you're exposed to pictures of thin models. However, if you have the genetic predisposition to misidentify food as a threat, then the exposure to pictures of thin models *may* indeed be one of several environmental factors that will activate the condition.

Evidence-based treatment

Many people are unaware that most treatments for an eating disorder are largely not evidence-based.

Evidence-based treatment requires that the following steps have been completed: 1) clinical trials where the treatment in question is measured against a control group and, 2) other researchers have duplicated the results. Ideally, the treatment has also been measured over a long period of time to further ensure the outcomes are not short-lived as well.

Today, only one treatment protocol qualifies as evidence-based treatment: Maudsley family-based treatment (FBT). FBT has controlled and duplicated trials along with published and confirmed five-year remission rates to support its classification as evidence-based treatment.

Two other protocols, Kartini (a family-based approach) and Mandometer (a technology-based approach), have self-published data but no independent corroboration of their findings as yet.

Problematically, FBT is specifically designed for child and adolescent sufferers of eating disorders and its design is difficult to translate into an adult patient environment.

Homeodynamic Recovery Method

The Homeodynamic Recovery Method is the set of science-based guidelines for recovery from an eating disorder that are published on the Eating Disorder Institute website. There have been no controlled trials or independent corroboration and therefore the Homeodynamic Recovery Method cannot be identified as evidence-based treatment at this point.

However, the guidelines are based on clinical trial data from FBT and the Minnesota Starvation Experiment, along with other published and peer-reviewed data, rather than merely being derived from empirical observation or practitioner philosophy. The name of the treatment program reflects the way in which the human body manages its own energy balance.

Homeodynamics is a way of viewing the human living system as defined by Martha Elizabeth Rogers (1914 - 1994) and is often called "nursing theory". The three principles of homeodynamics are that human nature is dynamic, ever-changing and holistic. Within the space of functional medicine, homeodynamics captures the reality that there is no one homeostatic optimal state for a living system, but rather a range that dynamically adjusts in response to internal and external stimuli.

The Homeodynamic Recovery Method for reaching remission from an eating disorder encompasses the fact that the human living system is optimized when most biological systems are actually running well above 100% and effectively clamped by key enzymes to remain at 100%. These clamping mechanisms are economical from an energy perspective rather than trying to rev the system up to be at 100% but no higher.

The Homeodynamic Recovery Method includes the following key facets:

1. Unrestricted eating with minimum intakes that are set to reflect actual average consumption of non-restricting equivalents[17]

2. No workouts or exercise, and no weighing or taking body measurements[†,18,19]

3. Applying specific training to address the misidentification of food as a threat[‡]

Additionally, an omnivorous diet is highly recommended, although an ovo-lacto vegetarian diet can be accommodated. Ultra-processed foods are encouraged in the early phases of recovery as explained in the post *Food, Family and Fear*, found on the Eating Disorder Institute website.[20]

Prevalence

One-third of all people who diet will end up on the eating disorder spectrum.[21,22]

While not all will develop clinical cases, if left untreated they will experience lifelong anxieties and compulsions around food and weight gain. The condition can develop into a clinical case at any point due to life stressors (anything from a cold to a break-up). Over time, those with the condition will often slide up and down the spectrum,

---

† Numerous inpatient environments resort to "blind weigh-ins" (standing on the scale backward) so that they can monitor the patient's progress while ensuring the patient is not triggered to relapse by knowing his or her weight. But the larger issue of why we must know our weight is overlooked in this approach. Weighing oneself is counterproductive to accepting that optimal weight set points are maintained without cognitive interference.

‡ The training involves synthesizing and practicing natural behavior that is at odds with the dominant cultural environments in which we live today. This will be explained further in chapter 6.

or express multiple facets of the spectrum at once (anorexia, restrict/ reactive eating cycles, bulimia, orthorexia [extreme focus on healthy foods], and anorexia athletica [over-exercise]).

Problematically, all clinical trials identifying the prevalence of eating disorders use the narrow, and largely unrepresentative, symptom checklists found in the DSM for identifying those with eating disorders.

When Dr. Daniel Le Grange and his colleagues reviewed and analyzed community-based surveys to uncover eating disorder prevalence, they offered the following conclusions:

Although the lifetime prevalence estimates of eating disorders from population-based studies of adults are relatively low (0.5% – 1.0% for anorexia nervosa [AN] and 0.5% – 3.0% for bulimia nervosa [BN])... community studies that used dimensional measures in youths have also yielded far greater prevalences of disordered eating behaviors (i.e., 14% – 22%) than those found in studies that applied strict DSM-IV diagnostic criteria.[23]

The prevalence of eating disorders in infertile women is also five times higher than the population-wide lifetime prevalence rate.[24] While you may have been used to seeing prevalence rates for distinct DSM categories that suggest lifetime rates of between 0.3% to 2%, as an entire spectrum disorder that can impact quality and length of life, it is conservative to apply the much broader range of 20% to 33%.

The reason for the disparity between diagnosed prevalence and community-based prevalence is two-fold: the DSM categories are narrow, and many with the condition are unaware their behaviors would constitute the presence of an eating disorder and thus never seek treatment.

Here are the criteria for diagnosing AN in the DSM-5:

- Persistent restriction of energy intake leading to significantly low body weight (in context of what is minimally expected for age, sex, developmental trajectory, and physical health)

- Either an intense fear of gaining weight or of becoming fat, or persistent behavior that interferes with weight gain (even though significantly low weight)

- Disturbance in the way one's body weight or shape is experienced, undue influence of body shape and weight on selfevaluation, or persistent lack of recognition of the seriousness of the current low body weight.[25]

As you can see from the above criteria, someone with a drive to be fit (and not thin) who spends significant amounts of time working out and attending to optimal macronutrient intake would not self-identify as having AN, nor would she receive such a diagnosis through psychiatric evaluation. However there is a classification in the DSM-5 called unspecified feeding or eating disorder (UFED) which will allow for a clinician to identify that a person is experiencing significant distress or impairment of quality of life due to eating or feeding behaviors that do not meet the exact criteria for AN, BN, etc. However in order for a patient to be diagnosed with an eating disorder she must first self-identify as experiencing distress and a reduction in quality of life such that she will seek psychiatric evaluation.

Given we live in a society where the pursuit of fitness and so-called healthy eating is unlikely to be seen as impairing quality of life (although it most certainly does for those with an eating disorder), a large number of those with active eating disorders remain unidentified and untreated in the community as their behaviors are almost indistinguishable from the accepted norm.

Within our current sociocultural fattist environment we need to ensure that we avoid underdiagnosis of eating disorders to avoid the commensurate harm that failing to diagnose and treat will entail for individual patients.

Statistics and prognosis

Between the ages of 15 and 24, eating disorders are 12 times more deadly than all other leading causes of death combined for that age group, including car accidents.[26]

The rates of remission range from 3% to 96% [27] and relapse rates range from 35% to 50%.[28,29] Remission rates for FBT at 12- and 36-month follow-ups are 75%.[30,31,32]

Standardized mortality ratios (SMRs) for eating disorders range from 1.92 to 10.5.[33,34,35] A standardized mortality ratio is a scientific way of identifying the increased risk of death associated with a particular condition when compared to a random healthy group of human beings. The standardized mortality ratio for a random healthy group is set at 1.00.

Because causes of death for those with eating disorders can range from heart failure to suicide, it is not always possible to extract accurate data if their underlying contributing condition (namely the eating disorder) is not identified on the death certificate. That is why

SMRs vary from one trial to the next. Reframing the SMR ranges into something more tangible, eating disorders have approximately a 1 in 4 to 1 in 5 fatality rate over a 20-year period.

The prognosis is that 50% will achieve full remission and generally maintain that remission, and the remaining 50% struggle with chronicity, social decline, progressive ill health, and early death.[36] This data applies no matter the treatment program applied.

Is an eating disorder a brain disease?

Before we get into the Homeodynamic Recovery Method as a treatment for eating disorders, I would like to further clarify the philosophy underpinning this approach a bit further. As mentioned in the previous section, psychiatrists diagnose eating disorders as they are currently classified as mental illnesses.

The first Diagnostic and Statistical Manual of Mental Disorders (DSM) identified asthma as mental illness, a classification that has of course been removed from subsequent versions of the DSM.[37] As we learn more about certain conditions, our understanding of them changes, or at least we hope it does. Yet in our eagerness to remove the stigma of mental illness, all manner of conditions of the mind are now referred to as diseases of the brain.

Progressive brain disease or progressive neurological conditions worsen over time. Alzheimer's would likely be the most well-known brain disease, and other examples include Huntington's, Parkinson's, Lou Gehrig's (ALS), and multiple sclerosis. Although starvation does cause brain damage, that damage is largely reversible through the re-feeding process to remission. Eating disorders are therefore not progressive diseases of the brain.

Multi-directional system

Let's take a parallel example of how the medical community developed an understanding of stomach ulcers to get a sense of what eating disorders really entail:

Until the 1980s, stomach ulcers (inflammation, ulceration, and destruction of the stomach lining) were believed to be due to untenable levels of stress or a poor response to tenable levels of stress. But then along came Australian researchers Drs. Barry Marshall and Robin Warren who fought long and hard to shift deep and abiding dogma within the medical community. They were able to prove that a spirochete (bacterium), *Helicobacter pylori*, was actually responsible for the onset and development of most stomach ulcers.[38]

Yet it took well over a decade for the screening for *H. pylori* to become commonplace within general practice when a patient complained of symptoms associated with the presence of a stomach ulcer. Investigation has shown (*see quote below*) that it normally takes an unacceptable amount of time to have clear, evidence-based interventions, that are confirmed as having value within the research community, subsequently adopted within the practitioner space.

The timing gap from the point at which something tangible has been determined by research to the point at which that tangible new diagnostic screening or treatment has been widely adopted by medical practitioners is very long. Drs. Russell Glasgow and Karen Emmons, while investigating the barriers that block translation of research breakthroughs into practitioner spaces, had the following to say regarding the state of this problem today:

Discrepancies between evidence-based, efficacious interventions and what actually occurs in practice are frequently so large as to be labeled a "chasm" by the Institute of Medicine. These gaps occur across prevention and disease management behaviors, and across settings, conditions, and population groups.[39]

But the saga of stomach ulcers does not end there. Although the identification and successful treatment of H. *pylori* resulted in a significant reduction of stomach-related cancers (it turned out an untreated *H. pylori* infection heightens the risk of such cancers), identification of specific susceptibility to these infections had the medical community circling back to the beginning. Both the exposure to unrelenting stressors and the presence of particular genetic predispositions must be present before *H. pylori* can take hold.[40]

While at this point a pathogen (infective agent) could not be ruled in or out when it comes to eating disorders, we most certainly can learn from what the parallel investigations of the causes of stomach ulcers have revealed.

The conditions listed in the DSM as mental disorders are identified with separate symptom checklists that bypass common genetic underpinnings. As just one example, bipolar disorder and schizophrenia are distinct conditions within the DSM, but genetic studies indicate these conditions are one and the same, based on proband and genotyping investigations.[41,42] Eating disorders are another example where proband, twin, and genotyping studies all confirm that discrete symptoms are merely variations of the same underlying genetically predisposed misidentification of food as a threat.[43,44]

Of course a genetic predisposition tells us nothing of the individual's likelihood of developing an active state of any of these conditions. Nor can we identify how the sociocultural, familial, and environmental factors will shape not only the activation of the condition, but also its expression and progression. Genetic predisposition also tells us nothing of how the condition may perseverate, worsen, or resolve to full remission.

And although stomach ulcers have a causative infective agent, and presumably eating disorders do not, the same multi-directional system of environmental inputs linked with genetic predispositions mean that there is never one single cause for the presence of an eating disorder.

Thus psychiatry, as a specialty, should be sidelined from the exclusive diagnosis and management of these conditions and instead the newer cross-disciplinary area of psycho-neuro-immuno-endocrinology (PNIE) should take up the research, examination, diagnosis, management, and resolution of these conditions.

Perhaps despite its own best efforts, psychiatry will indeed morph to become the field of PNIE. However, human beings cannot be treated in isolation from the community in which they reside, and that suggests anthropology should also be included: APNIE.

The interactions between the patient's psychological state, her sociocultural space, and her neurological, immune, and endocrine (hormone) functions will reinforce or ultimately change the expression of genes prone misidentify food as a threat.

The four Ws and an H

While patients must navigate the sil specialties today, the framework of the Method rests on an as-yet-to-be mains The questions who, what, when, where, symptom checklists, are the foundation of the Homeodynamic Recovery Method.

Identifying an eating disorder becomes a patient-driven exercise the moment she determines her quality of life does not meet her expectations due to the invasive interference of the restrictive behaviors on her life. Those five questions frame the unique specifics of the condition's expression and impact on the patient's life. The answers frame the psychotherapeutic options that will best suit the patient involved. We will look at those psychotherapeutic options in more depth in chapter 5.

The brain is a social organ, and it therefore physically changes with all APNIE inputs. These changes are rarely signs of disease. They occur constantly in each of us and predominantly create increased resilience in brain function and heighten overall individual survival. What we call learning is realized as physical changes within the brain.

Mental illness may be the result of progressive brain disease or it may be merely a transitory dip in function followed by increased function, or it might entail a shift into a chronic altered state of function.

...ing disorder a mental illness?

...omeone with an eating disorder is best described as impaired (more on this in chapter 2). Individuals with this condition rarely lose their connection to what is referred to as consensus, or consensus-based, reality.[45]

Consensus-based reality can, and often does, include many technically unreal thoughts that are held to be true by the majority. Therefore, there is majority agreement that those thoughts are sane. As one example, we do not classify those who believe in one all-seeing, all-knowing deity as insane, however that belief could not be said to be a sensory-based reality. Sensory-based reality—what we can identify through our senses—can cause all manner of cognitive contortions to try to single out someone with psychosis, who hears the voice of God, as needing treatment without inadvertently treating everyone with a belief in a god as well—hence the usefulness of using consensus-based reality as way to identify psychosis.

Those with eating disorders are usually well aware they have a problem, even if they are applying denial tactics to avoid having to come to terms with the problem. They are grounded in consensus-based reality. Starvation does cause significant cognitive impairment that parallels what we might see in patients with physical trauma to the brain; only rarely, due to severe starvation, will a patient develop psychotic breaks with reality and, in those rare cases, re-feeding will usually resolve the attack.

But even the judicious use of consensus reality to identify those who are mentally ill among those who are mentally healthy, this still represents a binary concept that does not reflect the continuum of mental states. We are used to thinking of ourselves as being well or sick, but at what point does refusing to use a public washroom reflect mental illness vs. culturally normative expressions of hygiene? How many times does hand washing in a single day reflect the presence of an obsessive-compulsive disorder (OCD)?

Mental states do not have a clear marker of wellness and illness and they are fluid and changing throughout our lives, even throughout a single day.

The foundation of the Homeodynamic Recovery Method is that the subjective assessment of quality of life defines the necessity of treatment. The label-first approach to identifying mental illness is not a defining factor for determining whether or not the Homeodynamic Recovery Method is applicable for a patient.

Assessing quality of life allows you to step outside the clinical straitjackets of specialization and labels to determine for yourself whether you have lost critical facets of your quality of life to the behaviors and compulsions that drive the way you live your day-to-day existence (as you define it).

Ultimately it does not matter where one draws a line in the sand to identify behaviors beyond that line as expressions of mental illness; the issue is not the definition, but the self-defined level of distress that accompanies the expression of those behaviors.

Starving brain afraid of food

Fundamentally, the misidentification of food as a threat in any animal is not conducive to supporting life. That fact alone will be a definitive marker of a severe reduction in quality of life.

Keep in mind that the vast majority of those with eating disorders do not identify the drive to restrict as a misidentification of food as a threat. The drive to misidentify food as a threat resides in areas of the brain to which the conscious mind has almost no access. This threat is actually experienced as the conscious mind's post-hoc evaluation (i.e., a guess) of why the patient is dealing with uncomfortable levels of arousal (anxiety, jitteriness, shallow breathing, twitchiness, clamminess, drive to move, etc.). I will explain how sociocultural frameworks shape these post-hoc evaluations in the following chapters.

Restoring energy balance within the body (through rest and re-feeding) most certainly resolves many starvation-generated behaviors, which can also include anxiety, paranoia, depression, withdrawal, and extremely labile (changing) emotional states. However, in the absence of proactive learning and practicing of non-restrictive behaviors, remission from this deadly chronic condition is unlikely.

The application of behavior change is somewhat comparable to a desensitization program for a patient who has developed a severe allergy to peanuts. With a peanut allergy, the immune system misidentifies the proteins found within that legume as dangerous and it mounts an extreme response to rid the system of the foreign invader. It is that immune response that is potentially fatal to the patient rather than the proteins within the peanut itself. Recent research to help those with severe peanut allergies, using peanut flour to incrementally retrain the immune system to lower its response to those proteins, has met with success.[46]

With an eating disorder, several areas distributed throughout the brain that are responsible for identifying environmental threats have misidentified food consumption as a threat. Retraining the threat identification system with various pyschotherapeutic treatment modalities has met with clinical success for both eating disorders and a host of other related anxiety disorders. I will address these treatment options in more detail in chapter 5.

Most importantly, as a chronic neurological condition, learning and practicing new and non-restrictive patterns improve both the symptoms and expression of an eating disorder within the mind and body. The question of whether the mind, or consciousness, is an artifact of brain function, or is inherently an expression of brain function, is not critical to answer for the purpose of understanding the value of retraining the mind in reaching complete remission from an eating disorder.

Clinicians and patients have wrongly assumed that labeling these conditions as genetic in origin would remove the stigma associated with having a mental illness.

In fact several studies have shown that people's responses are surprisingly more judgmental in their interactions when another's behavior is framed as genetic in origin, and less judgmental and more patient when the behavior is framed as the result of environmental conditions or situations the patient has faced in her past or is facing today.[47,48,49]

An eating disorder is treatable primarily because the brain is a social organ capable of structural changes due to factors that are both within and outside of the owner's control. The outcomes of such treatments are ultimately unpredictable precisely because not all of the influencing factors are modifiable.

However it is important to reinforce the fact that an energy-depleted brain cannot function at all. Therefore, in the absence of adequate rest and re-feeding to reverse the energy deficit in the body, moving an eating disorder toward remission will have no hope of success.

We will now take a more detailed look at how an eating disorder is experienced and expressed.

End Notes for Chapter One

1. Albert J. Stunkard, "Binge-Eating Disorder and Night-Eating Syndrome," in *Handbook of Obesity Treatment*, eds. Thomas A. Wadden and Albert J. Stunkard (New York: Guilford Press, 2002), 114-116.

2. Gwyneth Olwyn, "Part I: Binge Eating Disorder and Conflict of Interest" *Eating Disorder Institute* (paper), June 15, 2015, https://www.edinstitute.org/paper/2015/6/15/part-i-binge-eating-disorder-conflict-of-interest.

3. Gwyneth Olwyn, "Part II: What Does BED Really Look Like?" *Eating Disorder Institute* (paper), July 10, 2015, https://www.edinstitute.org/paper/2015/7/10/part-ii-what-does-bed-really-look-like.

4. Lisa Cosgrove, Sheldon Krimsky, Emily E. Wheeler, Jenesse Kaitz, Scott B. Greenspan, and Nicole L. DiPentima, "Tripartite Conflicts of Interest and High Stakes Patent Extensions in the DSM-5," *Psychotherapy and Psychosomatics* 83, no. 2 (2014): 106-113.

5. Gwyneth Olwyn, "Part I: Binge Eating Disorder & Conflict of Interest" *Eating Disorder Institute* (paper), June 15, 2015, https://www.edinstitute.org/paper/2015/6/15/part-i-binge-eating-disorder-conflict-of-interest.

6. Gwyneth Olwyn, "Part II: What Does BED Really Look Like?" *Eating Disorder Institute* (paper), July 10, 2015, https://www.edinstitute.org/paper/2015/7/10/part-ii-what-does-bed-really-look-like.

7. Lisa Cosgrove, Sheldon Krimsky, Manisha Vijayaraghavan, and Lisa Schneider, "Financial Ties between DSM-IV Panel Members and the Pharmaceutical Industry," *Psychotherapy and Psychosomatics* 75 (2006): 154-160.

8. Lisa Cosgrove, Sheldon Krimsky, Emily E. Wheeler, Jenesse Kaitz, Scott B. Greenspan, and Nicole L. DiPentima, "Tripartite Conflicts of Interest and High Stakes Patent Extensions in the DSM-5," *Psychotherapy and Psychosomatics* 83, no. 2 (2014): 106-113.

9. David H. Gleaves, Michael R. Lowe, Bradley A. Green, Michelle B. Cororve, and Tara L. Williams, "Do anorexia and bulimia nervosa occur on a continuum? A taxometric analysis," *Behavior Therapy* 31, no. 2 (2000): 195-219.

10. Kamryn T. Eddy, Pamela K. Keel, David J. Dorer, Sherrie S. Delinsky, Debra L. Franko, and David B. Herzog, "Longitudinal comparison of anorexia nervosa subtypes," *International Journal of Eating Disorders* 31, no. 2 (2002): 191-201.

11. Kamryn T. Eddy, David J. Dorer, Debra L. Franko, Kavita Tahilani, Heather Thompson-Brenner, and David B. Herzog, "Diagnostic Crossover in Anorexia Nervosa and Bulimia Nervosa: Implications for DSM-V," *American Journal of Psychiatry* 165, no. 2 (2008): 245-250.

12. Christopher G. Fairburn and Kristin Bohn, "Eating disorder NOS (EDNOS): an example of the troublesome "not otherwise specified" (NOS) category in DSM-IV," *Behaviour Research and Therapy* 43, no. 6 (2005): 691-701.

13. Shan Guisinger, "Adapted to Flee Famine: Adding an Evolutionary Perspective on Anorexia Nervosa," *Psychological Review* 110, no. 4 (2003): 745-761.

14. Janet L. Treasure and John B. Owen, "Intriguing links between animal behavior and anorexia nervosa," *International Journal of Eating Disorders* 21, no. 4 (1997): 307-311.

15. Walter H. Kaye, Guido K. Frank, Ursula F. Bailer, and Shannan E. Henry, "Neurobiology of anorexia nervosa: Clinical implications of alterations of the function of serotonin and other neuronal systems," *International Journal of Eating Disorders* 37, S1 (2005): S15-S19.

16. Ibid.

17. Gwyneth Olwyn, "Homeodynamic Recovery Method, Doubly-Labeled Water Method Trials and Temperament-Based Treatment" *Eating Disorder Institute* (papers), January 12, 2015, https://www.edinstitute.org/paper/2015/1/12/homeodynamic-recovery-method-doubly-labeled-water-method-trials-and-temperament-based-treatment.

18. Christie Zunker, James E. Mitchell, and Stephen A. Wonderlich, "Exercise interventions for women with anorexia nervosa: a review of the literature," *International Journal of Eating Disorders* 44, no. 7 (2011): 579-584.

19. Solfrid Bratland-Sanda, Jorunn Sundgot-Borgen, Øyvind Rø, Jan H. Rosenvinge, Asle Hoffart, and Egil W. Martinsen, ""I'm not physically active - I only go for walks": Physical activity in patients with long-standing eating disorders," *International Journal of Eating Disorders* 43, no. 1 (2010): 88-92.

20. Gwyneth Olwyn, "Food Fears 1: Food, Family and Fear" *Eating Disorder Institute* (blog), December 21, 2012, https://www.edinstitute.org/blog/2012/12/21/food-family-and-fear.html.

21. Jennifer M. Jones, Susan Bennett, Marion P. Olmsted, Margaret L. Lawson, and Gary Rodin, "Disordered eating attitudes and behaviours in teenaged girls: a school-based study," *Canadian Medical Association Journal* 165, no. 5 (2001): 547-552.

22. Catherine M. Shisslak, Marjorie Crago, and Linda S. Estes, "The spectrum of eating disturbances," *International Journal of Eating Disorders* 18, no. 3 (1995): 209-219.

23. Sonja A. Swanson, Scott J. Crow, Daniel Le Grange, Joel Swendsen, and Kathleen R. Merikangas, "Prevalence and correlates of eating disorders in adolescents: Results from the national comorbidity survey replication adolescent supplement," *Archives of General Psychiatry* 68, no. 7 (2011): 714-723.

24. Melissa Freizinger, Debra L. Franko, Marie Dacey, Barbara Okun, and Alice D. Domar, "The prevalence of eating disorders in infertile women," *Fertility and Sterility* 93, no. 1 (2010): 72-78.

25. "Classifying eating disorders - DSM-5" *Eating Disorders Victoria* (blog), June 19, 2015, https://www.eatingdisorders.org.au/eating-disorders/what-is-an-eating-disorder/classifying-eating-disorders/dsm-5.

26. Patrick F. Sullivan, "Mortality in anorexia nervosa," *American Journal of Psychiatry* 152, no. 7 (1995): 1073-1074.

27. Jennifer Couturier and James Lock, "What is remission in adolescent anorexia nervosa? A review of various conceptualizations and quantitative analysis," *International Journal of Eating Disorders* 39, no. 3 (2006): 175-183.

28. J. C. Carter, E. Blackmore, K. Sutandar-Pinnock, and D. B. Woodside, "Relapse in anorexia nervosa: a survival analysis," *Psychological Medicine* 34, no. 4 (2004): 671-679.

29. E.D. Eckert, K.A. Halmi, P. Marchi, W. Grove, R. Crosby, "Ten-year follow-up of anorexia nervosa: clinical course and outcome," *Psychological Medicine* 25, no. 1 (1995): 143-156.

30. Daniel le Grange, Ross D. Crosby, Paul J. Rathouz, and Bennett L. Leventhal, "A randomized controlled comparison of family-based treatment and supportive psychotherapy for adolescent bulimia nervosa," *Archives of General Psychiatry* 64, no. 9 (2007): 1049-1056.

31. James Lock, Daniel Le Grange, W. Stewart Agras, Ann Moye, Susan W. Bryson, and Booil Jo, "Randomized clinical trial comparing family-based treatment with adolescent-focused individual therapy for adolescents with anorexia nervosa," *Archives of General Psychiatry* 67, no. 10 (2010): 1025-1032.

32. Jon Arcelus, Alex J. Mitchell, Jackie Wales, and Søren Nielsen, "Mortality rates in patients with anorexia nervosa and other eating disorders: a meta-analysis of 36 studies," *Archives of General Psychiatry* 68, no. 7 (2011): 724-731.

33. Gunilla Paulson-Karlsson, Ingemar Engström, and Lauri Nevonen, "A pilot study of a family-based treatment for adolescent anorexia nervosa: 18- and 36-month follow-ups," *Eating Disorders: The Journal of Treatment & Prevention* 17, no. 1 (2009): 72-88.

34. Fotios C. Papadopoulos, Anders Ekbom, Lena Brandt, and Lisa Ekselius, "Excess mortality, causes of death and prognostic factors in anorexia nervosa," *The British Journal of Psychiatry* 194, no. 1 (2008): 10-17.

35. C. Laird Birmingham, Jenny Su, Julia A. Hlynsky, Elliot M. Goldner, and Min Gao, "The mortality rate from anorexia nervosa," *International Journal of Eating Disorders* 38, no. 2 (2005): 143-146.

36. Committee on Nomenclature and Statistics of the American Psychiatric Association, *Diagnostic and Statistical Manual Mental Disorders* (Washington DC: American Psychiatric Association, 1952), 6-30.

37. K. Tolstrup, M. Brinch, T. Isager, S. Nielsen, J. Nystrup, B. Severin, and N. S. Olesen, "Long-term outcome of 151 cases of anorexia nervosa," *Acta Psychiatrica Scandinavica* 71, no. 4 (1985): 380-387.

38. Barry J. Marshall and J. Robin Warren, "Unidentified curved bacilli in the stomach of patients with gastritis and peptic ulceration," *The Lancet* 323, no. 8390 (1984): 1311-1315.

39. Russell E. Glasgow and Karen M. Emmons, "How can we increase translation of research into practice? Types of evidence needed," *Annual Review of Public Health* 28 (2007): 413-433.

40. Mohammed Mahdy Khalifa, Radwa Raed Sharaf, and Ramy Karam Aziz, "Helicobacter pylori: a poor man's gut pathogen?" *Gut Pathology* 2, no. 1 (2010): 2.

41. J. A. Badner and E. S. Gershon, "Meta-analysis of whole-genome linkage scans of bipolar disorder and schizophrenia," *Molecular Psychiatry* 7, no. 4 (2002): 405-411.

42. Paul Lichtenstein, Benjamin H. Yip, Camilla Björk, Yudi Pawitan, Tyrone D. Cannon, Patrick F. Sullivan, and Christina M. Hultman, "Common genetic determinants of schizophrenia and bipolar disorder in Swedish families: a population-based study," *The Lancet* 373, no. 9659 (2009): 234-239.

43. Lisa R. Lilenfeld, Walter H. Kaye, Catherine G. Greeno, Kathleen R. Merikangas, Katherine Plotnicov, Christine Pollice, Radhika Rao, Michael Strober, Cynthia M. Bulik, and Linda Nagy, "A controlled family study of anorexia nervosa and bulimia nervosa: psychiatric disorders in first-degree relatives and effects of proband comorbidity," *Archives of General Psychiatry* 55, no. 7 (1998): 603-610.

44. Kelly L. Klump, K. B. Miller, P. K. Keel, M. McGue, and W. G. Iacono, "Genetic and environmental influences on anorexia nervosa syndromes in a population–based twin sample," *Psychological Medicine* 31, no. 4 (2001): 737-740.

45. Paris Williams, *Rethinking Madness: Towards a Paradigm Shift in Our Understanding and Treatment of Psychosis* (San Rafael, CA: Sky's Edge Publishing, 2012).

46. Pooja Varshney, Stacie M. Jones, Amy M. Scurlock, Tamara T. Perry, Alex Kemper, Pamela Steele, Anne Hiegel, Janet Kamilaris, Suzanne Carlisle, Xiaohong Yue, Mike Kulis, Laurent Pons, Brian Vickery, and A. Wesley Burks, "A randomized controlled study of peanut oral immunotherapy: Clinical desensitization and modulation of the allergic response," *The Journal of Allergy and Clinical Immunology* 127, no. 3 (2011): 654-660.

47. John Read, Nick Haslam, Liz Sayce, and Emma Davies, "Prejudice and schizophrenia: a review of the 'mental illness is an illness like any other' approach," *Acta Psychiatrica Scandinavica* 114, no. 5 (2006): 303-318.

48. Sandra Dietrich, Michael Beck, Bujana Bujantugs, Denis Kenzine, Herbert Matschinger, and Matthias C. Angermeyer, "The relationship between public causal beliefs and social distance toward mentally ill people," *Australian and New Zealand Journal of Psychiatry* 38, no. 5 (2004): 348-354.

49. John Read and Niki Harré, "The role of biological and genetic causal beliefs in the stigmatisation of 'mental patients'," *Journal of Mental Health* 10, no. 2 (2001): 223-235.

Chapter Two

The Embodied Eating Disorder

*Gwyneth: What surprised you most once you began recovery?
The worst and the best thing?*

Patient E: The worst surprise about recovery was just how pervasive fattism truly is, even in those who love you. My husband was so vehemently against recovery, and still is, because he sees my being fat as ruining my life. He refuses to accept that there was anything wrong with my behaviors, sadly because many of them are so much the norm these days. It was, and still is, extremely hurtful to me that even the man who promised to love and cherish me no matter what holds so much anger and prejudice directed at me about something I literally could do nothing about. And that my choice to recover the way I needed to was not acceptable because it would change the life he had become accustomed to, never mind that I was always miserable and unhappy stuck in the cycle that I was in.

The best surprise about recovery was that my judgment towards obese persons and obesity completely melted away. My heart opened up to people, because I understood that I could never truly understand what a person's struggles were just by looking at them. That what a person looks like is not a true measure of not only their health, but their worth. Really good things started to happen in my relationships with others during this transformation and my heart is much more full as a result.

Patient N: I think I was most surprised by how isolating recovery was, for a long time. Partly this was because I entered the process feeling sure I'd be one of the lucky ones who snap back within a matter of months, and I had no idea how painful and transformative a process it would turn out to be—and partly because I struggled to find appropriate support from a doctor or counselor, and I really floundered for a while. It still baffles me how little information there is out there about recovery experiences beyond the "recover but not too much" approach. It all started to feel slightly unreal, and it was difficult for friends and family to understand, too. In the end it was the fact that I was in touch with others in a similar boat that kept me going—that and the fact that despite the anxiety, I knew that eating enough and resting made sense, however hard it was. Recovery also made me realise that my relationship with food had been severely messed up for a lot longer than I first thought, and how hunger had loomed over me, breathing down my neck for a lifetime.

The nicest surprise was also how transformative recovery has been. It has changed me in ways I never imagined it would. I am still a long way from feeling physically "normal"—but I feel freer than I ever have. It is almost impossible to describe how amazing it is simply to feel at peace around food, and how calm my mind is without the cacophony of ED* noise. My concentration is almost unshakeable these days, and I feel at ease with myself in a way I never have before. I'm very fat and very stiff and swollen still, but things have really fallen into place this past year: I found a job I love, and have finally found a career path that excites me—something I didn't have the mental stamina or the passion for when my mind was governed by my eating disorder. I have a better relationship with my family and friends, and a level of quiet confidence in my abilities that only ever seemed fleeting before.

---

*   ED: eating disorder.

This chapter explores the experience of having an eating disorder in more detail. The condition is chronic and is experienced and lived throughout the entire mind and body.

Telltale dozen

How can you tell if you have an eating disorder? Because it is a neurobiological condition and therefore rarely includes external, visible symptoms; it is the mindset you are forced to adopt toward food that is most telling.

Those dealing with this condition are two-thirds more likely to be of average or above-average weight than the emaciated icon that is commonly used to represent the condition in our popular culture.[1] The fact that emaciation is not a definitive marker is yet another reason to pay particular attention to analyzing mindset, behaviors, and subjective reduction in quality of life.

1. Family and friends have shifted from congratulating you on your weight loss and/or your healthier choices to making either careful or even blunt comments that you look unwell and generally don't seem to eat enough. When workouts, runs, exercise and/or clean eating are dominant behaviors, then family and close friends start to make comments about how they feel you are unable to keep your commitments and priorities straight (meaning you put your behaviors ahead of your relationships).

2. You are cold when others are not. You've started wearing sweaters (jumpers, pullovers) when others are in short sleeves. Sometimes you feel light-headed or dizzy. Other times you feel foggy-headed—like you are listening to others through cotton wool.

3. You are tired and find your mind wanders. You struggle to focus in class or at work. You cannot remember things that others remember easily.

4. You are prone to crying spells and/or explosive bouts of anger (more so than what might be usual). You alternate between wanting to be alone, snapping at family, and finding you are clingy and needy, seeking reassurance from loved ones.

5. Not only do you find it hard to concentrate, but also you find you are absolutely consumed with thoughts of food: when you will eat; what you will eat; what you won't eat.

6. Facing social circumstances that involve food creates panic: family celebrations, lunches with friends at school, holiday gatherings…in the days leading up to such events you feel extremely anxious and spend a lot of time trying to figure out how to avoid it altogether.

7. The number of rules you assign to when and how will eat keeps getting longer. You have become ritualistic to the point where any deviance causes massive anxiety (the wrong plate, the fork in the wrong place…).

8. You have longer and longer lists of forbidden foods that you will not touch.

9. If you indulge in any food that you consider unacceptable, you are wracked with shame, self-hatred, and loathing and usually "punish" yourself for the transgression (exercising to exhaustion, skipping yet another meal).

10. As a woman[†], your regular menstrual cycle is irregular or has disappeared completely. Whether you are a woman or man you notice your skin appears dull and dry. Your hair and nails are brittle and perhaps your hair loss seems more pronounced than usual (clumps in the bathtub drains or on your brush).

11. You find yourself promising yourself and others more and more that tomorrow will be different. But it isn't.

12. You lie to loved ones about what you ate that day or how much you actually exercised and make excuses for why you cannot eat now. You may fabricate food allergies, intolerances, or other reasons why you cannot have the food being offered.

Why is the eating disorder mindset present?

When an eating disorder is activated, APNIE[‡] changes occur in the patient's mind and body that presumably do not occur for those who don't have the condition. Those changes and their exposure to various psychosocial and environmental reinforcements, make the telltale dozen feel like such a spiraling trap for those with an eating disorder.

[†] The absence of a menstrual cycle is a marker of ill health but its presence is not a marker of health. It is a one-way marker only.

[‡] APNIE: anthropologically-framed psycho-neuro-immuno endocrinology as explained in Chapter 1.

When people restrict food intake, or experience an energy deficit in their bodies for whatever reason, leptin levels plummet in the body. Leptin is a gating hormone that manages metabolism, appetite, bone formation, immune function, and reproductive hormone function.[2,3,4,5,6,7]

When a person is energy balanced, leptin is at an optimal level. When leptin levels plummet two things happen: the metabolism is suppressed and the appetite increases. Describing the process in this way is a gross oversimplification of the complex hormonal and neurotransmitter cascades that occur when a person lowers his or her food intake, but the explanation will suffice for the purpose of this overview.

For the person with an eating disorder, the appearance of an energy deficit presumably activates genes that affect normal function of neurotransmitters in the brain. It is these neurotransmitters that are believed to generate the anxious and compulsive thoughts, feelings, and behaviors around food.[8,9]

A woman without an eating disorder will say she feels irritated, fatigued, hungry, and moody when dieting. The lowered leptin level is creating unpleasant moods and extreme hunger to signal to the brain that it is time to go find more food to eat.

A person with an eating disorder will say she's not hungry. Although experts dispute whether she actually does feel hunger or not, it's clear she initially feels calmer, more energized, and dissociated from negative feelings (emotionally blunted) as a result of avoiding food intake.[10,11,12] The eating disorder–skewed neurotransmitters appear to interact with the lowered leptin level in a way that is distinct from the norm: the usually unpleasant moods are replaced with positive emotional outcomes (in the short term). Even as the irritation, mood swings, exhaustion, and deep hunger may begin to override that initial positive outcome of creating energy deficits in the body, now the brain's threat identification system is also locked into keeping food avoidance in place.

If someone essentially feels better when she avoids food, then that can be a powerful reinforcement to continue with the avoidance. Activation of an eating disorder should have a period in which either extinction or habituation might occur—meaning the avoidance behavior may or may not stick, depending on the presence of other positive or negative influences in the patient's life at that time. But it's quite likely that this window of opportunity is too short and too subtle to be accessible to tangible intervention.

Other researchers suggest that the perseveration of behaviors is not due to the positive mood modulation effect of starvation, but rather the pursuit of removing ambiguity through the application of rules.[13] But, as with almost everything to do with these complex neurological conditions, likely both the positive mood modulation due to neurotransmitter-based anomalies and the drive to avoid unpleasant arousal or ambiguity quickly allow food avoidance behaviors to take root. This conditioning will occur for those with the genetic underpinning who also face those necessary psychosocial inputs to reinforce and prolong the application of food avoidance behaviors.

What is really going on?

Most patients are profoundly puzzled when I inform them that their condition is essentially a misidentification of food as a threat. The common response is "But I'm not afraid of food, I just_____." The fill-in-the-blank usually includes fattist statements in one form or another but occasionally fat phobia is absent from the post-hoc explanations as well.

The prefrontal cortex in our brains, responsible for our conscious thought processes, is habitually underestimated for its imaginative and creative capability. It is perceived as the seat of logical thought and in Western culture that logical capability is considered the essence of human superiority. It is the prefrontal cortex that generates that fill-in-the-blank best guess *after the fact* when the internal system (both brain structures and the body as a whole) has been placed into a fight/flight/freeze state of arousal. The more accurate phrase would be: "I believe (fill-in-the-blank) *because* my threat identification system in my brain has typecast food as a threat."

Our threat identification system is a powerful system distributed throughout several brain structures that, evolutionarily speaking, are much older structures than our prefrontal cortex. We share part to all of this threat identification system with essentially all other animals on the planet.

Any brain structure responsible for our survival works with extreme efficiency and doesn't concern itself too much with accuracy. The threat identification system is our lightning-fast yet somewhat dirty system (reflecting that efficiency trumps accuracy for survival). Our prefrontal cortex, conversely, tries to concern itself more with accuracy and that means it ends up working as a slower yet cleaner system. The prefrontal cortex has little influence or neural oversight over the threat identification system. The way I view these complementary systems in our brain is that the evolutionarily older structures in our brain largely excuse and indulge the overblown sense of importance that our prefrontal cortex believes it has in running our lives.

If you are walking across a field and out of the corner of your eye you see a snake about to strike, the prefrontal cortex is blissfully uninvolved in all the reactions you enact to jump back to avoid the strike. However, once you are hopefully standing to the side watching the snake slither away, your prefrontal cortex will now consciously frame the experience that you were about to be bitten by a snake: "Whew! We avoided that one! Way to go, team!" Of course the rest of the brain that was really responsible for that lightning-quick response rolls its collective "eyes," knowing full well that the prefrontal cortex was most certainly not part of the team—it arrived late, as usual, and full of itself.

The exact same reaction can occur when out of the corner of your eye you see a stick on the ground that looks like a snake moving toward you. And when I say "you see," in fact the part of your brain registering what is coming in through the retina is really not accessible to the conscious "you" in the story. You will likely jump back immediately and full seconds may elapse before you (as in prefrontal cortex "you") recognize and confirm that it is just a stick. The prefrontal cortex then might sheepishly laugh but the rest of the brain responsible for that reaction doesn't care because it runs on a better-safe-than-sorry track. That is your fast-and-dirty neural processing system at its finest. That the stick was not a snake is an irrelevant error—efficient response, but not necessarily accurate.

Now let's get back to what is happening for the threat identification system in someone with an activated eating disorder.

Because eating disorders are essentially a type of anxiety disorder, they have close links to the kinds of neural responses we see in patients with both specific phobias as well as obsessive-compulsive disorder. In all expressions of anxiety disorders, the threat identification system is too sensitively calibrated or what I would call "twitchy."

How does this system become twitchy in the first place? Well, we can be born predisposed to have a sensitively calibrated threat response system. Both low cardiac vagal tone and high startle response at birth predisposes the individual to the development of anxiety disorders in later life.[14] However, much of the subsequent infant-mother postpartum interactions can greatly dampen or heighten these predispositions.[15,16]

There is also a fair amount of research data on the measurable differences in the serotonergic and dopaminergic systems in the brains of those with an eating disorder when compared to healthy controls.[17,18,19] These neurotransmitter systems are implicated in our reward identification system, which balances the threat identification system in our brain. The reward identification system, too, is distributed across several evolutionarily older brain structures.

Think of this process as: reward = approach, threat = avoid

When these two systems are well attuned, releases of neurotransmitters frame what types of things in our environment we want more of and what things we want less of. It creates a nice positive spiral of increased survival and improved quality of life.

While we know that there is dampened function of the reward identification system in those with eating disorders, this reduced activity may actually be the result of heightened threat identification responses dampening the reward system. In other words, the facets that researcher Walter Kaye investigates (serotonin and dopamine function[20]) may be the result of preexisting anomalous amygdala function (a brain structure that is intimately involved in threat identification). And anomalous amygdala function, perhaps combined with persistent low vagal tone and high startle responses, may subsequently all act upon the reward identification system to dampen its activity overall in the brain.

Walter Kaye and his colleagues have identified that anxiety disorders are a common precursor for the development of an eating disorder.[21] And while much of the neuroscientific focus on the study of anxiety rests with the amygdala-cortical interactions, the involvement of the orbitofrontal cortex is equally relevant and may also explain why sociocultural framing of mental illnesses change throughout history.

The frontal lobes are one of four main areas in our brains. Within the frontal lobes (left and right hemisphere) are three main areas: prefrontal cortex, the premotor area, and motor area. The orbitofrontal cortex resides within the prefrontal cortex, the area responsible for complex thought. The orbitofrontal cortex provides an important connection between the frontal lobes and the temporal lobes, where auditory, visual and emotional perceptions are interpreted. Our decision-making ability is inextricably linked to memory and emotional salience (importance).[22] The orbitofrontal cortex supports the complex decision-making skills that occur within the prefrontal cortex through its connection to the temporal lobes, where the entire limbic system resides.

In overly simplistic terms, the orbitofrontal cortex is bidirectional in its ability to receive messages from other structures in the brain as well as send messages to the amygdala. It scans your surrounding environment all the time. If it identifies a concern or threat, it communicates with the amygdala, an area within the brain's limbic system. However, the amygdala can also inform the orbitofrontal cortex that there are interoceptive (internal body) inputs that suggest a problem is present, and the orbitofrontal cortex is then instructed to scan the environment more closely for a likely source of the problem. This facet of the orbitofrontal cortex is likely why a patient with anorexia nervosa living in the 1700s explained her avoidance of food as an attempt to get closer to God and a patient with the same condition today states that she is avoiding food to stay "healthy," thin, and fit. In both cases there are interoceptive changes that activate the pattern to find the source of the problem in the surrounding environment. To make meaning of the internal distress, the mind latches onto dominant sociocultural norms.

If you are sitting in front of a plate of pasta and you are hungry, then you begin eating. But what if, along with hunger, your heart rate has increased, your hands are clammy, and your breathing is shallow? You are likely not even consciously aware just yet that your internal state is not relaxed. But soon the signals become more insistent. You feel jittery and you want to leave the table. You identify that you are anxious. At this point there is frantic firing between the amygdala and the orbitofrontal cortex creating a "Check again!" loop. The internal setting is most definitely suggesting there is a threat present and nearby, but the orbitofrontal cortex is scanning and sees a plate of pasta.

That's when the impasse reaches the conscious mind because there is no clear logical or identifiable threat. So the prefrontal cortex does what it does best: tries to make meaning of it all. And in the absence of any clear threat it will have to guess using its lifetime exposure to sociocultural and environmental inputs.

Patients do not experience food avoidance as the misidentification of food as a threat because the prefrontal cortex has to make meaning out of a nonsensical situation: "The plate of pasta cannot be a threat, so what am I missing?" In today's culture, a patient will likely frame the avoidance of food as concern for the types of ingredients in the pasta that may be "unhealthy" or perhaps worry that the amount of calories in the pasta will make her fat (and therefore socially abhorrent). And of course our patient back in the 17th century was framing her avoidance of pasta as an expression of religious adherence and godliness.

The threat identification and reward systems in the brain of someone with an eating disorder are misaligned or imbalanced, but experts cannot fully explain all the reasons why that happens or why it is food that gets miscast as a threat. Both our reward and threat identification systems work as positive feedback systems, so any imbalance between these two systems quickly spirals out of control. A reward identification system unleashed can lead to pathological levels of addiction. A threat identification system unleashed can lead to pathological levels of aversion.

For those with an eating disorder, an aversion to food is the fundamental life-threatening result of a threat identification system that has lost its way.

Can it be stopped early in its tracks?

Well, that will depend on what "it" is. An eating disorder usually has a very long prodrome. A prodrome is the period during which the condition is activated and there are observable symptoms but those symptoms sit below the threshold of full diagnosis.

We might even argue that an anxious four- or six-year-old may sit in a pre-prodrome state for an eating disorder. And in fact a selective eating disorder or picky eating (now classified as avoidant/restrictive food intake disorder [ARFID] within the DSM-5) from birth is a pre-prodrome state for an eating disorder.[23,24,25]

Most certainly a pre-prodrome state should allow for many interventions that could theoretically prevent the child entering the prodrome for an eating disorder by the time she hits puberty. By definition a pre-prodrome state means that the condition (in this case an eating disorder) is truly inactive.

A highly anxious child or extremely picky eater[§] could, with helpful age-appropriate guidance, learn to apply anxiety-easing techniques. An open trial showed that children aged seven to eight could be taught to apply mindfulness to ease anxiety.[26] And a randomized controlled trial of children ages 9 to 13 suggested that mindful attention training enhances social-emotional resiliency.[27]

---

§ The picky eating being referenced in this case is not the more common form of average cautious and fastidious eating seen in all young children. Picky eaters will have an extremely narrow number of foods that they are prepared to eat and will not succumb to multiple exposures of new foods (as will average cautious children).

And while the body of evidence for mindfulness training in young children is still being developed, the evidence so far is sufficiently promising that it is worth considering such interventions in children between the ages of six to nine. In other words, we cannot say that such interventions will ultimately remove the chance of subsequent activation of an eating disorder in the teen years, but it is theoretically possible, at that early stage, that sufficient anxiety modulation training may have preemptive power. I will explain mindfulness in more detail in chapter 5.

The prodrome may last several years before the patient reaches the threshold of clinical diagnosis for an eating disorder. When your 11-year-old girl has decided to forego desserts because she wants to eat better, or your 10-year-old boy wants to get rid of his potbelly by doing more sit-ups, or your child decides to become a vegetarian for ethical reasons, then you may be witnessing strong indicators your child is entering the eating disorder prodrome.

Meaningful intervention at this early juncture may be difficult for several reasons. First of all, not every prepubescent tween (ages 9–12) will progress toward an eating disorder simply because they adopt a vegetarian diet. Secondly, prepubescent tweens and pubescent young teens are beginning a natural individuation and maturation process, so what is interpreted as an experimental phase and what constitutes evidence of an ominous eating disorder prodrome will be indistinguishable to even the most attuned parent or involved adult. And thirdly, the reason an eating disorder takes hold and inexorably progresses is also due to the sociocultural feedback that confirms to the child that those behavior changes exhibit moral and mature decision-making.

Neither awareness nor prevention campaigns generate any measurable outcomes, but they appear to be the top-of-mind effort these days for most national and international eating disorder organizations. In fact you will be very hard pressed to find any value to these kinds of health awareness campaigns whatsoever. In one meta-analysis of numerous health awareness campaigns, the best outcome was for seat-belt usage. Seat-belt usage had an enforcement component (i.e., it was a fineable offense) and even that added impetus only resulted in a very modest outcome with an r~ value of 0.15.¶ [28]

If we look at the parallel efforts that have been made in awareness campaigns to halt the presence of both online and in-person bullying in school children, we find that what works is not what is usually applied. In a truly brilliant departure from the usual anti-bullying programs out there, middle schools in the state of New Jersey implemented an anonymous online survey. As expected, the perception was that bullying and pro-bullying attitudes were far more prevalent than was actually the case. From there, the researchers developed print media posters to convey the actual norms from the survey results. One poster example was "Did you know: 96% of us think we should always try to be friendly with students who are different from us?" Using a conformity-to-peers model, the researchers hoped that exposure to the print media would result in a commensurate reduction in all bullying measures. The percentage reduction in all bullying measures from the campaign across all schools averaged 16%. [29] In other words,

---

¶ A statistical value that shows a mere 15% change in behavior in seat belt usage could be attributed to the awareness campaigns.

just by pointing out to kids that the vast majority of them is not bullying others created a pressure to conform to that non-bullying norm for the bullies among them.

If we were serious about preemptive efforts with eating disorders in the young, then that is the kind of methodical effort that we would need to apply to ensure that the intervention actually generated desired results.

I suspect that conformity to peers is indeed the model that would be successful for preempting the reinforcement of food avoidance behaviors for those with the genetic and psychosocial predispositions to acquire and reinforce those behaviors. However, in a society in which we expect grade-school children to be weighed, know their body mass indices, recognize that foods can be classified as "bad" or "good," and make sure that they "exercise to stay healthy," conforming to the norm actually exacerbates the prevalence and severity of eating disorders in our schools.

For worried parents or school counselors, it is best to focus attention on inoculation rather than awareness or prevention. Teach children to question cultural norms and teach them scientific practice.

I remember when my son was in grade four and he was assigned a project to create an advertising campaign by picking a product that he liked and then amassing the imagery (clipping magazines) and writing the appropriate supportive copy. It was the perfect opportunity for the kids to learn a bit about advertising techniques and manipulation, and to get them thinking about how they felt and responded to the advertisements that they saw hundreds of times a day. But, apart from my own likely boring and judicious efforts to indoctrinate my son on how to be ad-savvy, nothing was covered in the classroom on that topic whatsoever.

Young people do not create youth culture or youth-obsessed culture; they consume it like the rest of us. Consumerism *is* our culture. How we dress, talk, behave and treat others is all framed within a marketing construct where the status we wish to achieve is almost exclusively defined through the products and services we consume. The power of a youthful brain (between the ages of 15 to 25 or so) is that if they are given the opportunity, they will turn their rebellious eyes towards unquestioning consumption in favor of generating not merely a culture that is truly theirs, but a culture that becomes ours as a whole. However, while as adults we micromanage all facets of our young peoples' lives these days, we fail to guide them towards critical thought and assessments of the world they will inherit. Inoculating a child that might be predisposed to developing an eating disorder will at least involve helping them develop a critical sense that the thinness ideal within advertising and media is designed to sell products and services and does not reflect an inherent pursuit of meaning or purpose as a human being.

By accepting the fattist attitudes in our society without any skeptical or scientific inquiry on your own part; by insisting that diet and exercise are valid for weight management and that it all equates to good health outcomes; and by assuming that those with eating disorders are just taking medically sound approaches of diet and exercise just a bit too far, you (as a parent, teacher, school counselor, or health care provider) are creating the environment that will maximize the chance your son or daughter, students, clients, or patients are too brittle to bend away from the predisposition they might have for developing an eating disorder.

As distressing and tragic as it is, it is realistic that we focus on what to do when an eating disorder has well and truly taken hold. It will be at that point, when the increasingly negative impacts on quality of life start to become hard to ignore that you, or your loved ones, will want to do something to reverse the trajectory altogether. I once explained the core facet of pursuing remission on the Eating Disorder Institute forums as follows:

Gwyneth - April 19, 2015

The thing you have to wrap your mind around is: [the fear is] not real.

Think of it like some sci-fi movie where you've been injected with a drug that will make you see horrific monsters all around you, but you were told beforehand that that is what the drug would do and you have to override what you are pretty sure you're seeing by holding onto the thought that the monsters are not real.

No matter what you think your reasons are for continuing to starve or exercise even when you know it's harming you badly, those reasons are a complete mirage. You are starving or exercising for absolutely no other reason beyond the fact that your brain's threat system is seeing monsters every time you try to eat and rest.

There's no magic to recovery. It's just eat, breathe and let the panic wash through you by reminding yourself: the fear's not real. I have to eat. I have to rest.**

** The Eating Disorder Institute forum post.

End Notes for Chapter Two

1. Melissa Whitelaw, Heather Gilbertson, Katherine J. Lee, Mick B. Creati, and Susan M. Sawyer, "A new phenotype of anorexia nervosa: the changing shape of eating disorders," *Journal of Eating Disorders* 1, suppl 1 (2013): O44.

2. F. Elefteriou, S. Takeda, K. Ebihara, J. Magre, N. Patano, C. Ae Kim, Y. Ogawa, X. Liu, S. M. Ware, W. J. Craigen, J. J. Robert, C. Vinson, K. Nakao, J. Capeau, and G. Karsenty, "Serum leptin level is a regulator of bone mass," *Proceedings of the National Academy of Sciences of the United States of America* 101, no. 9 (2004): 3258-3263.

3. Fortunata Carbone, Claudia La Rocca, and Giuseppe Matarese, "Immunological functions of leptin and adiponectin," *Biochimie* 94, no. 10 (2012): 2082-2088.

4. Jeffrey M. Friedman, "The Function of Leptin in Nutrition, Weight, and Physiology," *Nutrition Reviews* 60, suppl 10 (2002): S1-S14.

5. Simón Méndez-Ferrer and Paul S. Frenette, "Hematopoietic Stem Cell Trafficking," *Annals of the New York Academy of Sciences* 1116 (2007): 392-413.

6. Ursula Meier and Axel M. Gressner, "Endocrine Regulation of Energy Metabolism: Review of Pathobiochemical and Clinical Chemical Aspects of Leptin, Ghrelin, Adiponectin, and Resistin," *Clinical Chemistry* 50, no. 9 (2004): 1511-1525.

7. Ilona A. Barash, Clement C. Cheung, David S. Weigle, Hongping Ren, Emilia B. Kabigting, Joseph L. Kuijper, Donald K. Clifton, and Robert A. Steiner, "Leptin is a metabolic signal to the reproductive system," *Endocrinology* 137, no. 7 (1996): 3144-3147.

8. Walter H. Kaye, Guido K. Frank, Ursula F. Bailer, Shannan E. Henry, Carolyn C. Meltzer, Julie C. Price, Chester A. Mathis, and Angela Wagner, "Serotonin alterations in anorexia and bulimia nervosa: new insights from imaging studies," *Physiology & Behavior* 85 (2005): 73-81.

9. F. Fumeron, D. Betoulle, R. Aubert, B. Herbeth, G. Siest, and D. Rigaud, "Association of a functional 5-HT transporter gene polymorphism with anorexia nervosa and food intake," *Molecular Psychiatry* 6, no. 1 (2001): 9-10.

10. Shan Guisinger, "Adapted to flee famine: Adding an evolutionary perspective on anorexia nervosa," *Psychological Review* 110, no. 4 (2003): 745-761.

11. Ester M. S. Espeset, Kjersti S. Gulliksen, Ragnfrid H. S. Nordbø, Finn Skårderud, and Arne Holte, "The Link Between Negative Emotions and Eating Disorder Behaviour in Patients with Anorexia Nervosa," *European Eating Disorders Review* 20, no. 6 (2012): 451-460.

12. Kathleen Mary Berg, Dermot J. Hurley, James A. McSherry, and Nancy E. Strange, *Eating Disorders: A Patient-Centered Approach* (Oxon, UK: Radcliffe Medical Press, 2002).

13. Rhonda M. Merwin, C. Alix Timko, Ashley A. Moskovich, Krista Konrad Ingle, Cynthia M. Bulik, and Nancy L. Zucker, "Psychological inflexibility and symptom expression in anorexia nervosa," *Eating Disorders: The Journal of Treatment & Prevention* 19, no. 1 (2011): 62-82.

14. Theodore Beauchaine, "Vagal tone, development, and Gray's motivational theory: toward an integrated model of autonomic nervous system functioning in psychopathology," *Development and Psychopathology* 13, no. 2 (2001): 183-214.

15. Christin L Porter, "Coregulation in mother-infant dyads: Links to infants' cardiac vagal tone," *Psychological Reports* 92, no. 1 (2003): 307-319.

16. Christin L. Porter, Melissa Wouden-Miller, Staci Shizuko Silva, and Adrienne Earnest Porter, "Marital Harmony and Conflict: Links to Infants' Emotional Regulation and Cardiac Vagal Tone," *Infancy* 4, no. 2 (2003): 297-307.

17. Walter H. Kaye, Julie L. Fudge, and Martin Paulus, "New insights into symptoms and neurocircuit function of anorexia nervosa," *Nature Reviews Neuroscience* 10, no. 8 (2009): 573-584.

18. Walter H. Kaye, Guido K.W. Frank, and Claire McConaha, "Altered dopamine activity after recovery from restricting-type anorexia nervosa," *Neuropsychopharmacology* 21, no. 4 (1999): 503-506.

19. Guido K. Frank, Ursula F. Bailer, Shannan E. Henry, Wayne Drevets, Carolyn C. Meltzer, Julie C. Price, Chester A. Mathis, Angela Wagner, Jessica Hoge, Scott Ziolko, Nicole Barbarich-Marsteller, Lisa Weissfeld, and Walter H. Kaye, "Increased Dopamine D2/D3 Receptor Binding After Recovery from Anorexia Nervosa Measured by Positron Emission Tomography and [11C]Raclopride," *Biological Psychiatry* 58, no. 11 (2005): 908-912.

20. Walter H. Kaye, Julie L. Fudge, and Martin Paulus, "New insights into symptoms and neurocircuit function of anorexia nervosa," *Nature Reviews Neuroscience* 10, no. 8 (2009): 573-584.

21. Walter H. Kaye, Cynthia M. Bulik, Laura Thornton, Nicole Barbarich, Kim Masters, and Price Foundation Collaborative Group, "Comorbidity of anxiety disorders with anorexia and bulimia nervosa," *American Journal of Psychiatry* 161, no. 12 (2004): 2215-2221.

22. Antoine Bechara, Hanna Damasio, and Antonio R. Damasio, "Emotion, decision making and the orbitofrontal cortex," *Cerebral Cortex* 10, no. 3 (2000): 295-307.

23. Corinna Jacobi, W. Stewart Agras, Susan Bryson, and Lawrence D. Hammer, "Behavioral validation, precursors, and concomitants of picky eating in childhood," *Journal of the American Academy of Child & Adolescent Psychiatry* 42, no. 1 (2003): 76-84.

24. Anthony J. Mascola, Susan W. Bryson, and W. Stewart Agras, "Picky eating during childhood: A longitudinal study to age 11 years," *Eating Behaviors* 11, no. 4 (2010): 253-257.

25. Gwyneth Olwyn, "Part IV-A UCSD EDC2014 Review" *Eating Disorder Institute* (conferences), January 25, 2015, https://www.edinstitute.org/conference/2015/1/25/part-iv-a-ucsd-edc2014-review.

26. Randye J. Semple, Elizabeth F. G. Reid, and Lisa Miller, "Treating Anxiety With Mindfulness: An Open Trial of Mindfulness Training for Anxious Children," *Journal of Cognitive Psychotherapy* 19, no. 4 (2005): 379-392.

27. Randye J. Semple, Jennifer Lee, Dinelia Rosa, and Lisa F. Miller, "A Randomized Trial of Mindfulness-Based Cognitive Therapy for Children: Promoting Mindful Attention to Enhance Social-Emotional Resiliency in Children," *Journal of Child and Family Studies* 19, no. 2 (2010): 218-229.

28. L. B. Snyder, M. A. Hamilton, E. W. Mitchel, J. Kiwanuka-Tondo, F. Fleming-Milici, D. Proctor, "A Meta-Analysis of the Effect of Mediated Health Communication Campaigns on Behavior Change in the United States," *Journal of Health Communication: International Perspectives* 9, suppl 1 (2004): 71-96.

29. H. Wesley Perkins, David W. Craig, and Jessica M. Perkins, "Using social norms to reduce bullying: A research intervention among adolescents in five middle schools," *Group Processes & Intergroup Relations* 14, no. 5 (2011): 703-722.

Chapter Three

Science-Based Treatment for an Eating Disorder

Patient P: The main thing that has changed is my relationship with my kids. About 2 months into recovery I began to feel emotions again and I remember the exact month I finally fell in love with my kids. I am so ashamed to say that before then I was pretty much a zombie. I looked after them and loved them as best as I could but I can see now that I was really skimming the surface of what kind of parenting experience I could offer. In fact, I always believed I was a terrible mother, cold and harsh. It has been an absolute joy to find as the months have gone on that I am in fact a very loving, patient and kind person...I just couldn't show it. An eye opening moment for me was reading something that Brene Brown wrote – (paraphrasing) "You cannot selectively numb the bad feelings like anger, sadness, frustration without also numbing the good feelings like joy, love, happiness"... And it is so true.

I was numb to everything, even the birth of my children. I can remember holding each of my children and it was as if I was on the periphery of the scene looking in at this little family, not knowing what to feel...

I think that love is the reason I have kept going through all of the sheer horribleness. I love myself too much now to go back. And I know that might sound trite, I don't mean it to at all. It's just that my life was so devoid of love that to have been gifted with it at almost 40 years old is the most amazing experience. I feel like I've been given a second chance at life. The other reason I have kept going is that I have a group of absolutely amazingly patient and generous women on Uzilu†† who have helped me pick my way through mental traumas, the difficulties that recovery has brought and taken me by the internet hand at times and helped me find strength I didn't know I had, shown me the beauty I could not see in myself when I was panicking and just generally offered support on a day to day basis. I would not have made it this far without journalling or the input from my recovery friends. You cannot underestimate, either, the gift of knowing that other people are going through the same stuff and have come out of the other side.

The Homeodynamic Recovery Method is founded on research outcomes from two key sources: the Minnesota starvation experiment and Maudsley family-based treatment (FBT). Beyond that, the method also comprises the synthesis of countless peer-reviewed published research papers on the neurobiological expression, medical biomarkers, and outcomes that can confirm the presence or absence of full remission from this chronic condition.

---

†† Uzilu.com is an online forum space that began when the Eating Disorder Institute forums were on hiatus in 2012 and it continues alongside the Eating Disorder Institute supporting those going through the Homeodynamic Recovery Method to reach remission from an eating disorder.

Minnesota Starvation Experiment

In 1944, as the ravages of starvation due to World War II were at their peak across Europe, a researcher sought to gain an understanding of the physiological impacts of starvation and re-feeding in the hopes that it might be possible to help survivors restore their health.

Dr. Ancel Keys, responsible for the development of the US army's *K*-rations and head of the laboratory of physiological hygiene at the University of Minnesota, believed that a study on starvation might have important humanitarian and practical benefits. Keys enlisted 36 volunteers for his starvation experiment. They were all young male volunteers who formed part of the Civilian Public Service as conscientious objectors.

The first 12 weeks involved standardizing the men on 3200 kilocalories per day (kcal/day) while assessing all their biological and psychological markers as a baseline prior to the semi-starvation period of the study. Three months in, the calorie intake was cut to 1570 kcal/day. The diet was carbohydrate rich and protein poor to simulate the conditions faced by many in war-ravaged Europe. During this six-month semi-starvation period the physical and psychological impacts of the restriction were astounding to Keys and his fellow researchers.

There are numerous online sources that provide a comprehensive outline of the experiment and its outcomes, and a good book on the topic is *The Great Starvation Experiment: Ancel Keys and the men who starved for science*, by Todd Tucker [University Minnesota Press, 2006].

For the purpose of the development of the Homeodynamic Recovery Method for treating an eating disorder, there are two critical outcomes from the Minnesota starvation experiment that form self-evident yet nonetheless greatly overlooked requirements for reaching remission after self-imposed restriction of food intake: 1) a starved brain works very poorly; and 2) excess food intake will be required beyond pre-starvation amounts to restore weight, health, and ultimately sanity.

Dr. Emily Troscianko, a researcher in the field of eating disorders, had the following analysis to offer on how the Minnesota starvation experiment informs the recovery process from an eating disorder:

1. *If you regain weight, not only the physical effects of your current state — being constantly cold and weak, sleeping and concentrating poorly, bad hair and skin — will disappear, but so will the ways in which you currently think and feel. Your body is starved, and your character and your thoughts are dominated by this starvation, and will cease to be so once you allow yourself to regain weight.*

2. *There is no point in waiting for the magical moment at which you decide, once and for all, that you want to start eating more again, or to regain weight. Your starved state is making you unable to think flexibly enough to fully comprehend the possibility of eating or living differently, or even the possibility of wanting to think about and enjoy things other than food; it has hidden from you who you really are, and made you believe you are nothing but the anorexia; it is making the smallest piece of food feel like too much. For these reasons you will never truly want to recover, but you have to seize all your feelings of despair, desperation, hope, recklessness, and curiosity in order to make yourself plunge into*

that first day and first meal of recovery. As long as you keep yourself going, keep eating, through the first difficult weeks, it will get easier and easier.[1]

As with a patient suffering from suboptimal blood oxygen levels (hypoxia), or a patient suffering from diabetic-induced combativeness (in need of insulin), or even a patient who has head trauma involving potentially fatal injury assuring the paramedics he is fine, the brain is not designed to identify its own impairment. There is a reason that anti–drinking-and-driving campaigns urge you to make plans to have an alternate way of getting home *before* you head out for a night on the town: by the time you have had a couple of drinks you will not be able to correctly assess the fact that you are too impaired to drive safely.

There are still recalcitrant and dogmatic old-school format treatments for eating disorders that emphasize the need for neutralizing the influence of supposedly cold and distant mothers, for psychodynamic analysis, and for insisting that self-imposed starvation is not about the food. However, fortunately most modern and science-based treatments have recognized that, until a patient is re-feeding and redressing the energy deficits, the brain cannot function. Therefore, expressions of psychological distress may well be present entirely due to the starvation-induced impairment of the brain—exactly as was seen in the Minnesota starvation subjects.

No one takes too much issue with the rather self-evident necessity of re-feeding after a period of self-imposed starvation. Where things get awfully sticky is that *excess* food intake is actually required to redress the energy deficit in the body. In chapter 1, I explained how the research chasm reflects the serious delay from the time at which there is sufficient clinical trial data to change practice behaviors, to the actual point at which those behaviors are dependably and broadly in place in practitioner settings. The research chasm is at work for the treatment of eating disorders precisely because the research data confirm excess energy will be required to reverse the impacts of starvation and yet many treatment programs still apply food intake guidelines that are only relevant for those without eating disorders.

Overshooting fat mass in weight restoration

The model predicted that the fat mass overshoot was not permanent… however, recovery of the original body composition was predicted to take more than a year. The predicted mechanism of the fat mass overshoot was an enhanced rate of de novo lipogenesis in the early re-feeding period, followed by a dramatic increase of fat intake during ad libitum feeding.[2]

In its original published form, the Minnesota starvation experiment comprises two volumes. The above quote is from an in-depth computational analysis of the masses of data provided by that starvation experiment. Another similar computational review of the same starvation data restated the same outcome as follows: *"the original body weight and composition was eventually recovered but body fat mass was predicted to take more than one additional year to return to within 5% of its original value."* [3]

If there is one phrase that strikes cold, icy fear into the heart of any self-respecting, weight-conscious person today it is *"fat mass overshoot…"* In fact they will stop reading after the word *overshoot…* or maybe even at the word *fat*.

But what is this dreaded overshoot really all about? And maybe it appeared for a bunch of hapless volunteers in a starvation study that would be too unethical to replicate today, but surely it is different when it comes to re-feeding from a period of self-imposed starvation due to an eating disorder?

It is the curse of the research chasm that "recover, but not too much" prevails in too many treatment programs ostensibly designed to help patients with an eating disorder reach remission. Treatment decisions such as assigning specific weight targets or body mass index points, indicating that there is a risk of developing binge eating, and/or suggesting that the overshoot of fat mass is dangerous or unhealthy all contradict solid evidence that re-feeding after a period of semi-starvation involves eating to excess for a period of time. And for many, the recovery process will naturally involve a temporary, and needed, overshoot of fat mass for perhaps a year to several years before that fat mass naturally returns to its optimal point.

While these facts are not news within the research community, you can be sure that many practitioners will raise a skeptical eyebrow at the concept. To reach remission you must allow the body its process of energy replenishment as it sees fit.

Restriction is the enemy.

Restorative eating is designed to redress deficits

Drs. David M. Garner and Paul E. Garfinkel, researchers in the field of eating disorders responsible for developing numerous psychometric tests for the identification of eating disorder behaviors in individuals, had the following to say on the topic of the kind of reactive eating that was witnessed in the ad libitum (freely, without restraint) re-feeding period that occurred after the initial slow stepped re-feeding period in the Minnesota starvation experiment:

During the weekends in particular, some of the men found it difficult to stop eating. Their daily intake commonly ranged between 8,000 and 10,000 calories…

After about 5 months of refeeding, the majority of the men reported some normalization of their eating patterns, but for some the extreme overconsumption persisted: **"No. 108 would eat and eat until he could hardly swallow any more and then he felt like eating half an hour later"** *(p. 847). More than 8 months after renourishment began, most men had returned to normal eating patterns; however, a few were still eating abnormal amounts:* **"No. 9 ate about 25 percent more than his pre-starvation amount; once he started to reduce but got so hungry he could not stand it"** *(p. 847)… Serious binge eating developed in a subgroup of men, and this tendency persisted in some cases for months after free access to food was reintroduced; however, the majority of men reported gradually returning to eating normal amounts of food after about 5 months of refeeding. Thus, the fact that binge eating was experimentally produced in some of these normal young men should temper speculations about primary psychological disturbances as the cause of binge eating in patients with eating disorders. These findings are supported by a large body of research indicating that habitual dieters display marked overcompensation in eating behavior that is similar to the binge eating observed in eating disorders (Polivy & Herman, 1985, 1987; Wardle & Beinart, 1981).* **[emphasis mine].**[4]

Abdul Dulloo and his colleagues in 1997 postulated that the fat mass to fat-free mass data collected from the Minnesota starvation experiment during the ad libitum re-feeding period suggests *"that poststarvation hyperphagia [excess eating] is determined to a large extent by the autoregulatory feedback mechanisms from both fat and lean tissues."* The subjects all returned to pre-starvation fat mass to fat-free mass ratios, although, as mentioned above, it could take beyond a year for that to occur.[5]

Interestingly, a few clinical trials assessing the body fat composition of weight-restored patients with an eating disorder suggest that fat mass levels were higher than healthy controls and they remained unevenly distributed at the abdominal and tricep regions after re-feeding.[6,7] However, I suggest that this data is the result of incomplete recovery processes whereby a specific weight target was applied as a faulty marker of remission. If ad libitum re-feeding and longitudinal assessment are applied beyond the one-year period of weight readjustment, then in fact the clinical findings support my assessment: namely those with eating disorders also return to optimal fat mass to fat-free mass ratios assuming they mimic the re-feeding process seen within the Minnesota starvation experiment (i.e., they respond fully to hyperphagia).[8]

Restriction of food intake is very similar to restriction of sleep. The impacts of doing so are cumulative in nature. If you stayed up for 36 hours straight and then went to sleep, would you be concerned if your sleep lasted more than 8 hours? Would you be surprised if you were still tired when you awoke and the subsequent night you found you still required perhaps more sleep than was usual to feel really "caught up" the next morning?

Dieting is equivalent to sleep deprivation

The exposure to electric light has destructively impacted human sleep since its invention. The physiological and medical implications of chronic sleep deprivation on human populations are fairly well understood and yet, as a culture, we still tend to adhere to Thomas Edison's moralizing attitude that sleeping is a character flaw denoting weakness and lack of commitment.

Most people overeat 100 percent, and oversleep 100 percent, because they like it. That extra 100 percent makes them unhealthy and inefficient.[9]

And while this quote likely resonates with many reading this passage today, the fact of the matter is Edison knew nothing of physiology, biology, neurochemistry, or anything to do with the human living system. Drs. Jeffrey Durmer and David Dinges, both sleep medicine specialists, have confirmed in one of their studies that we adapt to sleepiness even as the cognitive impacts mount:

Recent chronic partial sleep deprivation experiments, which more closely replicate sleep loss in society, demonstrate that profound neuro-cognitive deficits accumulate over time in the face of subjective adaptation to the sensation of sleepiness.[10]

Just as we are capable of a subjective adaptation to the sensation of sleepiness, we can also develop a subjective adaptation to the sensation of hunger. In the face of this kind of practiced override to basic survival instincts, we doggedly continue to apply moralistic denial of biologic necessity.

And in case you weren't aware, scientists have actually confirmed that the reason you have prolonged sleep on weekends is indeed due to a reduction of sleep during the workdays.[11] Sleep deprivation is cumulative, as is the damage it causes to your body.

Partial sleep deprivation reduces the activity of natural killer cells in our bodies, impacts cortisol and melatonin levels, increases insulin resistance and diabetes mellitus type 2 onset, lowers leptin levels, increases risk of coronary heart disease, and increases the risk of certain kinds of cancers.[12,13,14,15,16,17,18,19,20,21] And that doesn't even cover the impacts of partial sleep deprivation on cognitive and motor functions!

You might be willing to accept that sleep deprivation is indeed harmful to your health. You may even be considering the possibility that feeling morally superior about suppressing your need for sleep is somewhat counterproductive to your long-term health outcomes, too.

Ah, but once we turn our attention to food a myriad highly unscientific cultural idiocies persist.

Weight set point theory

The word "theory" is used in everyday language to suggest that magical and unbelievable things could possibly exist. To say: "theoretically, the spaghetti monster exists," merely suggests that we lack sufficient sensory or measuring apparatus to be able to definitively prove or disprove the existence of the spaghetti monster.

The word "theory" in science does not mean that magical and unbelievable things could exist if only we had the sensory or measuring apparatus to prove or disprove their existence. A theory in science is a testable statement. That the human body maintains an inherited weight set point is an observable and measurable fact. We have yet to identify all the ways in which the human body protects its inherited optimal weight and that is why this observable state is posited as scientific theory.

Human height, weight, and body mass index are highly heritable. Classic twin studies indicate heritability of 0.80, 0.81, and 0.84 respectively.[22] A more detailed twin cohort study of the heritability of height across eight countries revealed that the heritability for women varied more than for men (0.68 to 0.84).[23]

It is a fact our bodies do maintain the inherited optimal weight very closely and various adipocyte- (cells within the fat organ) generated hormones and central nervous system feedback loops are implicated in the way in which the body protects its weight.[24,25,26,27,28,29]

That the body's autoregulation systems are elastic in nature is also true. Our body temperature has a range in which it operates well. It fluctuates naturally throughout the day. It can rise above the norm as a defensive measure against a pathogen (i.e., a fever) or drop below the norm to attempt to maintain core body temperature for survival (when exposed to very cold weather). However, as we know, these defensive maneuvers for temperature regulation can only manage so much external pressure—we can die from an extremely high fever or hypothermia.

Similar flexibility is present in the way that the largest hormone-producing organ in our bodies protects metabolic function. Fat is not a body tissue or an energy storage unit; it is the largest and centrally critical hormone-producing organ in your body.[30]

It is common nonsense that a fat organ enlarges beyond its optimal size because we eat more and move less.[31,32] As with body temperature regulation, the fat organ is normally elastic within a range of perhaps ±5–12 lbs. (± 2.3–5.4 kg). Of course that does not occur within a single day, but within weeks or months.

The fat organ also has defensive responses to external threats, just as does body temperature regulation. And while we may possibly eat more and move less when the body is under threat, those behaviors are not the causative inputs for an increase in size of the fat organ. I discuss these facts in significantly more detail in the Eating Disorder Institute papers under the category of obesity. For now, consider doing your own research on the causative impacts of sleep deprivation, unrelenting and unresolved life stressors, income inequality, exposure to endocrine disruptors, and the presence of an underlying metabolic condition to explain the threat responses of fat.

No healthy weight range

Weight, like height, is a bell-shaped curve, and someone has to hold down the upper standard deviation from the average, although few women accept this fact…Most media promote an unhealthy thinness or impossibly lean muscularity. The narrow range suggested by insurance company tables or other charts for individual weights are often used inaccurately. These weights are averages, not norms.[33]

Drs. Mehler and Andersen, quoted above, are right. Few people will accept that their optimal weight set point is not to the left of the peak on that bell-shaped curve, meaning they all want lower-than-average weight compared to the vast majority of the population who has an average weight. As we viciously discriminate against those with above-average weight in our society, it is not surprising that most wish to be lower-than-average weight.

The so-called healthy weight range of body mass index (BMI) 18 to 24.9 is not healthy by any standard measure of morbidity (ill health) or mortality (early death). In fact, the range that would more accurately apply as clinically healthier than expected is BMI 25–30.[34] However, as weight is a highly heritable trait, it is your inherited optimal weight set point that correlates with your actual individual health status. BMI can only be linked to ill health and death on a population-wide level and that data simply doesn't translate down to the individual level. If you have an inherited optimal weight set point that places you at BMI 30, then you will be profoundly energy depleted and progressively disabled, when trying to maintain a BMI of 24.

I have witnessed dozens of patients communicate on the Eating Disorder Institute forums that they would rather suffer the massive negative health, social, and emotional consequences of their eating disorder, or outright be dead, than be fat. Indeed. They are only expressing what is the norm in our society.

People would rather be dead than fat. In a poll run by Esquire magazine, two-thirds of respondents said they would rather be stupid or mean than fat. At least 54% said they would rather be run over by a truck than be extremely fat.[35]

As an exercise, just replace the word fat in the above quote, with the words *homosexual* or *black*. If you find that the exercise changes your prior unquestioning attitudes of hating fat, then you are on the right track.

Approximately 2% to 4% of the adult population will naturally sit in the BMI range of 18.5 to 20.9. Inherited pediatric thinness has a prevalence of 5% to 7%.[36] Natural thinness drops slightly from childhood to adulthood. Here are two important points to absorb on these BMI range facts:

1. An individual can only experience the potential of optimal health at his or her inherited optimal weight set point.

2. The chance that an adult will naturally have a BMI of less than 21 is less than 5%. The chance that an adolescent will naturally have a BMI of less than 21 is less than 8%.

To assign weight restoration levels at between BMI 18.5 to 20.9 for those in recovery from an eating disorder will force 92% (or more) of patients to continue to restrict intake and apply extreme activity, or other equally damaging compensatory behaviors, in a vain attempt to maintain a weight that is neither an inherited nor healthy state for them.

Long-term weight loss maintenance is so unattainable as to be an oxymoron. Virtually everyone who attempts to adjust an optimal weight set point downward (i.e., lose weight) will fail utterly within two years.[37]

Another solid meta-analysis showed that the best-case outcomes for sustained weight loss (no matter the program involved) was to regain 77% of initial weight lost by year four or five. And the remaining subjects enrolled were not even able to achieve that underwhelming result: they regained more than 77% of initial weight lost.[38]

But wait, in 2000 the National Weight Control Registry contained 2500 names of individuals who had lost an average of 72 lbs. (33 kg) and maintained that loss for five years. Given that at least 90 million people would have been dieting in the United States in 1995 (34% of its population[‡‡] five years before the 2500 successful weight losers were included in that registry), then actual long-term weight loss was successful for 0.003% of the population in the United States at that time.

It is therefore scientifically sound to reject specific weight restoration amounts or body mass index level of any kind when undergoing re-feeding from an eating disorder.

From Minnesota to Maudsley

The Minnesota starvation experiment provides us with the following incontrovertible and scientifically agreed-upon data for re-feeding after a period of self-imposed restriction of food intake:

1. Restricting food intake generates significant physical and psychological impairments. The undernourished brain is incapable of identifying its own impairment. The impairment usually resolves with re-feeding.

---

‡‡ That is the lowest percentage in the assessment range of 34–50% of the population as dieting in any given year, [source: MarketData 2012].

2. Re-feeding must be compensatory and unhindered for an optimal weight and fat mass to fat-free mass ratio to be realized.

3. For some, there is an overshoot in fat mass that may take more than one year to resolve to its optimal state.

4. Extreme hyperphagia (excess eating) will occur for many months and is symptomatic of energy depletion and not the onset of binge-eating behaviors.

Now let's look briefly at the only evidence-based treatment protocol for eating disorders out there today, FBT, and see how it can be applied outside of child-oriented treatment.

The history of this treatment approach dates back to the 1970s at the Institute of Psychiatry at the Maudsley Hospital in London, England. This was at the same period in history when renowned psychiatrist Hilde Bruch had just published her authoritative book on the presumed causes of anorexia in young girls: *The Golden Cage: The Enigma of Anorexia Nervosa* [Harvard University Press, 1978]. FBT could not be further removed from the science-free zone in which Hilde Bruch worked at the time.

FBT is, as I've stated, the only evidence-based treatment program available to those with eating disorders. Conversely Hilde Bruch merely surmised that the cause of eating disorders was essentially bad mothering in one form or another. As I have already discussed in previous chapters, childhood experiences of any kind do not cause eating disorders.

That is not to say that everyone with an eating disorder is free of traumatic or miserable childhoods. And in some cases the pursuit of remission from an eating disorder may require parallel counseling to address and resolve painful childhood experiences and traumas. However, keep in mind that a starved brain is not a working brain and so counseling will have little positive traction in the absence of re-feeding and re-energizing the body.

Fully 60% of the patients visiting the Eating Disorder Institute website for information on how to recover from an eating disorder are 24 years and older. This demographic is not currently supported within the FBT framework, hence the development of Homeodynamic Recovery Method.

Central to FBT is the construct that reversing the energy deficit within a child or adolescent with an active eating disorder is step one. FBT is "an intensive outpatient treatment where parents play an active and positive role."[39] FBT's first step coincides with the first and second legs of the three-legged stool of the Homeodynamic Recovery Method: weight restoration and repair of physical damage (through rest and re-feeding). We will look at the three-legged stool of recovery in more detail in the following chapter.

A starved brain is not a working brain. Much of the distress present for the patient will naturally lessen as the brain is provided with enough energy to function. Within FBT the initial responsibility for adequate rest and re-feeding is transferred entirely to the parents. However as the patient progresses through treatment, FBT's steps two and three are designed to help the patient regain control over his or her own healthcare decisions and to receive sufficient psycho-educational guidance such that the patient will return to maturational and developmental norms.

Returning children to these norms is the dominant approach in child psychology today. The tenet of this approach is that chronic mental and physical illness may cause a child or teen to veer from age-appropriate developmental markers but that all children and teens have a natural pull toward returning to such norms. Therefore the role of a child psychologist is to support and help the patient find his or her way back to age-appropriate maturity and growth. The Homeodynamic Recovery Method reflects how FBT might be redesigned to suit adult populations with eating disorders.

For most adults with active an eating disorder, the condition was initially activated at some point in childhood. The condition is genetic in origin, but its activation and perseveration in each individual involve innumerable environmental inputs that are invariably unique to each person.

For adult patients, they might have deviated from maturational and developmental norms when their condition was first activated in childhood and they might not have ever returned to a normative state in the intervening years to adulthood; or they might have experienced remission and a normative state fleetingly only to regress upon the condition's reactivation at some point; or they might have managed to navigate a subclinical eating disorder allowing for most developmental and maturational markers to have been achieved in an age-appropriate fashion, but they are now struggling to reach ongoing adult developmental markers.

In other words, each adult patient may or may not face the need to undergo some form of catch-up childhood and adolescent maturation. However all adult patients need to address how pervasively integrated their eating behaviors have become with their coping mechanisms and interactions with others as a whole, *and how the pervasiveness of these behaviors has knocked them from their own developmental arc as adults.*

Unlike children and teens with a recently activated eating disorder, many adults cannot connect to a time in which they lived without applying food avoidance behaviors in one form or another. Even when they think back to perhaps very young years when they ate "normally," that recollection is distinct from a memory linked to self-as-adult. That disconnect is why leaders in the field of eating disorder research, such as Dr. Tim Walsh, are working now towards disentangling how habits form as a way to try to realize better treatment outcomes for adults.[40]

While our biological maturation is complete at around age 25, humans are social primates whereby their brains develop and are structurally modified in response to environmental inputs throughout their entire lives. The most common impact that any serious chronic illness will have on an adult is that it invariably narrows the variety and intensity of environmental inputs that allow for normative levels of brain modification and development. While it is true that the rate of maturation and development in adulthood is not nearly as steep as what we see up to the age of 25, the presence of an eating disorder inexorably pushes an adult from her developmental arc.

The Homeodynamic Recovery Method has developed lockstep with my continual review and synthesis of the scientific material on eating disorders and it is no more a static treatment protocol than is FBT. But at no point in time has the Homeodynamic Recovery Method not included an equivalent to FBT's steps one, two and three. The third leg of the Homeodynamic Recovery Method is psychoeducational support and guidance, i.e. counseling and therapy. Psychoeducational guidance to help nudge a patient back to adult developmental norms is foundational to the Homeodynamic Recovery Method. We use the analogy of a sturdy three-legged stool to explain the three non-negotiable elements for applying the Homeodynamic Recovery Method: re-feeding, resting and brain re-training (i.e. psychoeducational guidance and support).

As we know, much of the anxiety associated with the Homeodynamic Recovery Method is that it actually spells out minimum intake guidelines matched to age, sex and height-based healthy control intake levels that have been confirmed with doubly labeled water trial method results (see chapter 4 for more detail). Many sink so much intellectual energy into disbelief surrounding the necessity of resting and re-feeding to *those* intake levels when it comes to lay person third parties who review the Homeodynamic Recovery Method, that the third leg of the three-legged stool that supports the Homeodynamic Recovery Method is often ignored.

Most adult treatment options for eating disorders within residential treatment settings tend to overlook that evidence-based treatment for children and adolescents requires an initial focus on rest and re-feeding with subsequent psychoeducational guidance. In other words, starvation-impacted adults are expected to benefit from psychoeducational guidance in the absence of adequate rest and re-feeding in many residential treatment settings. The insistence within the Homeodynamic Recovery Method model that resting and re-feeding must form part of the treatment alongside psycho-educational guidance is counter to dominant unscientific models of treatment for adults with eating disorders. As such, the contention that re-feeding and resting aren't integral to reaching remission for an adult, and yet are when you are a child with the same condition, has no scientific evidence to support it.

When a person develops influenza, there are some basic treatments that are universal to all of us that offer our immune system its best chance at overcoming the virus. Equivalently, the basics of re-feeding and resting for treating an eating disorder are universal. Imagine if we suggested children and teens with the flu should rest, drink plenty of fluids and seek medical intervention if fever and dehydration get out of hand, but that adults should "visualize their well state" and that will ensure their return to health. Adult humans are not silicon-based life forms from another planet. They actually have extremely close and overlapping needs for supporting life as is required in their immature progeny.

The psychoeducational guidance necessary to return to a normative developmental arc needs to be tailored for the individual. Psycho-educational guidance does not replace the need to rest and re-feed, nor does resting and re-feeding replace the necessity of psychoeducational guidance. Remember the three "R's" of remission: re-feed, rest and re-train—the sturdy three-legged stool.

The 3 R's are framed within the FBT model as: 1) handover the responsibility of re-feeding and resting to the parents; 2) incrementally transfer that responsibility back to the child as the treatment progresses to reflect a return to developmental norms; and throughout the process 3) provide the entire family (and patient in particular) with sufficient and tailored psychoeducational guidance such that remission can be achieved and sustained.

And this FBT model is reflected in the Homeodynamic Recovery Method model as follows: rest and re-feed in a structured way that would mimic how a parent would help a child return to an energy-balanced state and in such a way that the energy deficit can be rectified and the physical damage throughout the body repaired (FBT: 1 and 2); and seek sufficient psychoeducational guidance to uncover the ingrained nature of restriction in both coping and human interaction strategies that have resulted in reducing or halting a natural adult developmental arc, followed by learning and practicing the techniques specific to your needs that increase resilience in coping strategies and broaden natural and needed human interactions to return you to your optimal adult developmental arc (FBT: 3).

And it's also a good idea to remember that the three-legged stool to remission develops the right patina and becomes increasingly comfortable, if it is used regularly. Remission is practiced and is not a "one-time and done" destination.

While the Minnesota Starvation Experiment and the Maudsley FBT program inspired the framework of the Homeodynamic Recovery Method, the remainder of the scientific peer-reviewed and published material used to develop the Homeodynamic Recovery Method will be revealed in subsequent chapters examining the method in greater detail.

End Notes for Chapter Three

1. Emily T. Troscianko, "Starvation study shows that recovery from anorexia is possible only by regaining weight" *Psychology Today* (blog), November 23, 2010, https://www.psychologytoday.com/blog/hunger-artist/201011/starvation-study-shows-recovery-anorexia-is-possible-only-regaining-weight.

2. Kevin D. Hall and Vickie E. Baracos, "Computational modeling of cancer cachexia," *Current Opinion in Clinical Nutrition & Metabolic Care* 11, no. 3 (2008): 214-221.

3. Kevin D. Hall, "Computational biology of in vivo human energy metabolism during semi-starvation and re-feeding," *The FASEB Journal* 20, suppl A1300 (2006).

4. *Handbook of Treatment for Eating Disorders*, eds. David M. Garner and Paul E. Garfinkel (New York: Guilford Press, 1997), 156-157.

5. Abdul G. Dulloo, Jean Jacquet, and Lucien Girardier, "Poststarvation hyperphagia and body fat overshooting in humans: a role for feedback signals from lean and fat tissues," *The American Journal of Clinical Nutrition* 65, no. 3 (1997): 717-723.

6. Laurel Mayer, B. Timothy Walsh, Richard N. Pierson, Steven B. Heymsfield, Dympna Gallagher, Jack Wang, Michael K. Parides et al., "Body fat redistribution after weight gain in women with anorexia nervosa," *The American Journal of Clinical Nutrition* 81, no. 6 (2005): 1286-1291.

7. L. Scalfi, A. Polito, L. Bianchi, M. Marra, A. Caldara, E. Nicolai, and F. Contaldo, "Body composition changes in patients with anorexia nervosa after complete weight recovery," *European Journal of Clinical Nutrition* 56, no. 1 (2002): 15-20.

8. Laurel E. S. Mayer, Diane A. Klein, Elizabeth Black, Evelyn Attia, Wei Shen, Xiangling Mao, Dikoma C. Shungu, Mark Punyanita, Dympna Gallagher, Jack Wang, Steven B. Heymsfield, Joy Hirsch, Henry N. Ginsberg, and B. Timothy Walsh, "Adipose tissue distribution after weight restoration and weight maintenance in women with anorexia nervosa," *The American Journal of Clinical Nutrition* 90, no. 5 (2009): 1132-1137.

9. Thomas Alva Edison, *The diary and sundry observations of Thomas Alva Edison*, ed. Dagobert D. Runes and (New York: Greenwood Press, 1968), 178.

10. Jeffrey S. Durmer and David F. Dinges, "Neurocognitive consequences of sleep deprivation," *Seminars in Neurology* 25, no. 1 (2005): 117-129.

11. Pablo Valdez, Candelaria Ramírez, and Aída García, "Delaying and Extending Sleep During Weekends: Sleep Recovery or Circadian Effect?" *Chronobiology International* 13, no. 3 (1996): 191-198.

12. Michael Irwin, Anne Mascovich, J. Christian Gillin, Robert Willoughby, Jennifer Pike, and Tom L. Smith, "Partial sleep deprivation reduces natural killer cell activity in humans," *Psychosomatic Medicine* 56, no. 6 (1994): 493-498.

13. Ibid.

14. Michael R. Irwin, Minge Wang, Denise Ribeiro, Hyong Jin Cho, Richard Olmstead, Elizabeth Crabb Breen, Otoniel Martinez-Maza, and Steve Cole, "Sleep loss activates cellular inflammatory signaling," *Biological Psychiatry* 64, no. 6 (2008): 538-540.

15. Esther Donga, Marieke van Dijk, J. Gert van Dijk, Nienke R. Biermasz, Gert-Jan Lammers, Klaas W. van Kralingen, Eleonara PM Corssmit, and Johannes A. Romijn, "A Single Night of Partial Sleep Deprivation Induces Insulin Resistance in Multiple Metabolic Pathways in Healthy Subjects," *The Journal of Clinical Endocrinology & Metabolism* 95, no. 6 (2010): 2963-2968.

16. Kristen L. Knutson, "Sleep duration and cardiometabolic risk: a review of the epidemiologic evidence," *Best Practice & Research Clinical Endocrinology & Metabolism* 24, no. 5 (2010): 731-743.

17. Slobodanka Pejovic, Alexandros N. Vgontzas, Maria Basta, Marina Tsaoussoglou, Emmanuel Zoumakis, Angeliki Vgontzas, Edward O. Bixler, and George P. Chrousos, "Leptin and hunger levels in young healthy adults after one night of sleep loss," *Journal of Sleep Research* 19, no. 4 (2010): 552-558.

18. Hans K. Meier-Ewert, Paul M. Ridker, Nader Rifai, Meredith M. Regan, Nick J. Price, David F. Dinges, and Janet M. Mullington, "Effect of sleep loss on C-reactive protein, an inflammatory marker of cardiovascular risk," *Journal of the American College of Cardiology* 43, no. 4 (2004): 678-683.

19. Richard G. Stevens, David E. Blask, George C. Brainard, Johnni Hansen, Steven W. Lockley, Ignacio Provencio, Mark S. Rea, and Leslie Reinlib, "Meeting Report: The Role of Environmental Lighting and Circadian Disruption in Cancer and Other Diseases," *Environmental Health Perspectives* 115, no. 9 (2007): 1357-1362.

20. David E. Blask, "Melatonin, sleep disturbance and cancer risk," *Sleep Medicine Reviews* 13, no. 4 (2009): 257-264.

21. Richard G. Stevens, "Light-at-night, circadian disruption and breast cancer: assessment of existing evidence," *International Journal of Epidemiology* 38, no. 4 (2009): 963-970.

22. Albert J. Stunkard, Terryl T. Foch, and Zdenek Hrubec, "A Twin Study of Human Obesity," *JAMA* 256, no. 1 (1986): 51-54.

23. Karri Silventoinen, Sampo Sammalisto, Markus Perola, Dorret I. Boomsma, Belinda K. Cornes, Chayna Davis, Leo Dunkel, Marlies de Langea, Jennifer R. Harrisa, Jacob V.B. Hjelmborga, Michelle Lucianoa, Nicholas G. Martina, Jakob Mortensena, Lorenza Nisticòa, Nancy L. Pedersena, Axel Skytthea, Tim D. Spectora, Maria Antonietta Stazia, Gonneke Willemsena, and Jaakko Kaprio, "Heritability of Adult Body Height: A Comparative Study of Twin Cohorts in Eight Countries," *Twin Research* 6, no. 5 (2003): 399-408.

24. L. Girardier, "Autoregulation of body weight and body composition in man. A systematic approach through models and simulation," *Archives Internationales de Physiologie, de Biochimie et de Biophysique* 102, no. 4 (1994): A23-A35.

25. D. Joe Millward and D. G. N. G. Wijesinghe, "Energy partitioning and the regulation of body weight–Reply by Millward & Wijesinghe," *British Journal of Nutrition* 79, no. 1 (1998): 111-113.

26. J. J. G. Hillebrand, D. De Wied, and R. A. H. Adan, "Neuropeptides, food intake and body weight regulation: a hypothalamic focus," *Peptides* 23, no. 12 (2002): 2283-2306.

27. R. Cancello, A. Tounian, Ch Poitou, and K Clément, "Adiposity signals, genetic and body weight regulation in humans," *Diabetes & Metabolism* 30, no. 3 (2004): 215-227.

28. Hans-Rudolf Berthoud, "Multiple neural systems controlling food intake and body weight," *Neuroscience & Biobehavioral Reviews* 26, no. 4 (2002): 393-428.

29. Joel K. Elmquist, Roberto Coppari, Nina Balthasar, Masumi Ichinose, and Bradford B. Lowell, "Identifying hypothalamic pathways controlling food intake, body weight, and glucose homeostasis," *The Journal of Comparative Neurology* 493, no. 1 (2005): 63-71.

30. Gwyneth Olwyn, "Part I: Systematic Review of Weight Gain Correlates in Literature" *Eating Disorder Institute* (paper), January 21, 2015, https://www.edinstitute.org/paper/2015/1/21/part-i-systematic-review-of-weight-gain-correlates-in-literature.

31. Gwyneth Olwyn, "Part II: Systematic Review of Weight Gain Correlates in Literature" *Eating Disorder Institute* (paper), February 26, 2015, https://www.edinstitute.org/paper/2015/2/26/part-ii-systematic-review-of-weight-gain-correlates-in-literature.

32. Philip S. Mehler and Arnold E. Andersen, *Eating Disorders: a Guide to Medical Care and Complications*, second edition (Baltimore: John Hopkins University Press, 2010).

33. Katherine M. Flegal, Barry I. Graubard, David F. Williamson, and Mitchell H. Gail, "Excess Deaths Associated With Underweight, Overweight, and Obesity," *JAMA* 293, no. 15 (2005): 1861-1867.

34. L. Vincent, "The myth of an obesity epidemic," *News24*, last modified April 21, 2012, http://www.news24.com/Archives/City-Press/The-myth-of-an-obesity-epidemic-20150429.

35. Katriina L. Whitaker, Martin J. Jarvis, David Boniface, and Jane Wardle, "The Intergenerational Transmission of Thinness," *Archives of Pediatrics & Adolescent Medicine* 165, no. 10 (2011): 900-905.

36. Suzanne W. Fletcher, J. E. Buring, S. N. Goodman, A. G. Goodridge, H. A. Guthrie, D. W. Hagan, B. Kafka, C.M. Leevy, J.G. Nuckolls, A.B. Schneider et al., "Methods for Voluntary Weight Loss and Control," *Annals of Internal Medicine* 119, 7 part 2 (1993): 764-770.

37. James W. Anderson, Elizabeth C. Konz, Robert C. Frederich, and Constance L. Wood, "Long-term weight-loss maintenance: a meta-analysis of US studies," *The American Journal of Clinical Nutrition* 74, no. 5 (2001): 579-584.

38. John S. LaRosa, "U.S. Weight Loss Market Worth $60.9 Billion," *PRweb.com*, last modified May 9, 2011, http://www.prweb.com/releases/2011/5/prweb8393658.htm.

39. Daniel Le Grange and James Lock, "Family-based Treatment of Adolescent Anorexia Nervosa: *The Maudsley Approach*," Maudsley Parents, accessed January 1, 2010, http://www.maudsleyparents.org/whatismaudsley.html.

40. B. Timothy Walsh, "The Enigmatic Persistence of Anorexia Nervosa," *American Journal of Psychiatry* 170, no. 5 (2013): 477-484.

Chapter Four

Homeodynamic Recovery Method in Detail

April 12, 2012 - Blue Dolphin

After about two weeks of recovery I'm feeling overwhelmed and need a bit of reassurance. I am 35 and have struggled with bulimia and anorexia for over two decades. Finally started the attempts at 2500 per day this week after lurking around the site and gaining inspiration...

Currently, I'm feeling so awful with what I look like and the bloating in my stomach looks like I'm pregnant, my arms and face are puffy and my legs are aching horribly...not sure how much is water and how much is fat gain. I'm so embarrassed by how I look since it happened so quickly I am terrified my colleagues are going to make comments as they always commented on my size being small. My chest appears huge and I just don't recognize myself in the mirror...often I cry when I catch a glimpse of myself...I refuse to step on a scale as I know it will send me into relapse.

...I am so ashamed of my body right now and after most of my life fighting to stay slim it feels like failure despite knowing that this is actually part of the success. I guess I could just use some reassurance that the weight will even out at some point and I'll make it through this to peace...finally...right now I am so scared, so depressed and feeling

hopeless that recovery can happen. I really want to get through this and get healthy...after years of half hearted recovery attempts and hospitals this is the first real try I've made but it's also the most overwhelming of any of the attempts. It seems like just one minute at a time...I miss me (but was it ever really me anyway?).*

I remember having pneumonia and the doctor informing me that for my age I should expect to get back to normal in six weeks' time. I should have known better than to treat such a pronouncement as written in stone, and when I was still flaked out and exhausted two months in, I most certainly considered the possibility that something "was not normal."

Our bodies are not machines. There are no mechanisms and no binary concepts of working or not working (with the exception of alive or dead, of course). Think of your body more as an ecosystem.

Imagine you are a forest, or a desert, or tundra, or perhaps a swamp. The absolute health and resilience of a forest or a desert are not measurable because each ecosystem has multivariate inputs. I can count the number of species; I can count the number of invasive species; I can measure temperatures, water levels, humidity, air pressure; I can identify which species seem healthy and which seem stressed; and I can even study these items over seasons and times to see if trends emerge. But none of those measurements will tell me the state of health and resiliency of the entire system.

When Mount St. Helens in Washington State (US) erupted in 1980, generating spectacular vertical and lateral explosions, a deadly pyroclastic flow, and subsequent landslides, it flattened an area of

---

*   Posted on The Eating Disorder Institute forums.

about 22 by 12 miles (35 by 20 km). Jimmy Carter, the US president at the time, was said to have described it as a moonscape when he flew over to inspect the damage. Scientific predictions initially suggested the area would take generations to recover. However, within just three years, 90% of the original species were found to be growing within the blast zone.[1]

I use Mount St. Helens as an analogy for understanding two things about your body:

1. Symptoms and screening tests will never accurately identify overall resilience, or lack thereof.

2. What seems catastrophic may merely be a blip toward a new level of resilience.

Do not treat the Homeodynamic Recovery Method as a recipe or a set of exacting steps that will realize unequivocal and successful results. There are no assurances for any recovery effort, including this method.

Do not panic if you find some symptoms are not present, or seem to appear, disappear, and re-appear. Your entire recovery process may take you into full remission in as little as 3 months or as long as 79 months. The literature on time to remission is all over the map because there are no commonly agreed-upon definitions of remission for eating disorders at this time.

Three months is exceedingly rare. The median time to remission ranges from 14.4 months to 27 months.[2,3] And in some studies the physical aspects of remission are disengaged from the psychological aspects. Drs. James Lock and Jennifer Couturier identified that the mean time to physical remission was 11.3 months, but the mean time to register remission on eating disordered thoughts and behaviors (using the Eating Disorder Examination score as the measurement tool) was 22.6 months.[4] One longitudinal study spanning 10–15 years noted that time to remission was protracted—ranging 57–79 months, depending on the definition of remission.[5]

Some perceived recovery as coping with emotions, while others experienced themselves as healthier than people in general regarding food and weight. Different aspects were emphasized as important for recovery.[6]

The above quote originates from the abstract of a paper specifically identifying how patients perceive the state of remission, and I think it is by far the best model to apply to your own recovery process. I know from experience that patients want concrete numbers: "Do I reach remission in 14 months or 79 months, based on my history of restriction?" The very disappointing answer to that question sounds like a riddle, but it is nonetheless ultimately true: "The recovery process is entirely what you make of it and is utterly unique for you."

Pay attention to the small markers of progress along the way and celebrate them, rather than focusing on some imagined end state.

Like the post-eruption world around Mount St. Helens, your foundational goal in entering remission is to embrace a "new normal." If you maintain an eating disorder–generated focus on eating the right foods at the right time, hitting and maintaining a certain weight, gaining to restore fertility, restoring enough weight to get people off your back, or restoring enough weight to lessen symptoms of starvation, then you are going to miss the forest for the trees.

Your mission, when pursuing remission, is to relish your new resilience and to live a life beyond an identity that has been tragically narrowed to numbers on a scale, or mileage on a pedometer, or shape in a mirror, or managing your anxiety with behaviors that impair your quality of life.

Recover fast or slow?

A recovery process is not without rare but potentially fatal risks. It's not fair or accurate to assign these risks to the recovery process itself, because the brittleness of the living system has been caused by ongoing restriction.

No matter what facet of an eating disorder has had you in its grip (avoiding food, cycling through avoiding and reactively eating, using laxatives, diuretics and purging, applying exercise regimes to manage the anxiety of food intake, using prescription or illicit drugs to maintain a level of food avoidance that eases anxiety, or applying rigid concepts of so-called healthy diets and "pure" food choices) your current state has become akin to a well-crafted wizard doll I once received as a gift.

The doll stood perhaps 18 inches (46 cm) in height and it had been designed with pale leather, wood fashioned for the staff, hand-stitching, the odd semiprecious stone, and white furs for the robes, hooded cloak, and boots, with white hair and beard—not a jolly Santa type; a wizard. The details were exquisite but I knew nothing of maintaining leathers and furs. Everything became brittle and fragile over time. As long as he was never touched or moved, he seemed fine. But move him, or try to deal with accumulating dust, and he shed as explosively as a cat visiting the vet. He still looked beautiful, but on close inspection the cracked, stressed leather and dull fur became apparent.

The conundrum with recovery from an eating disorder is that a go-low-and-slow approach to re-feeding has no clinical evidence to support its use,[7,8] but it is still often applied because common sense would suggest that trying to take the brittle, faded wizard back to a lustrous and resilient new state requires gingerly curating the restoration process. But as you already know, common sense is often nonsense when it comes to the ever-present research chasm. "Go low and slow" is the phrase often used to describe keeping a patient at low intake amounts and slowly increasing her intake over an extended period of time.

An eating disorder is, at its core, an anxiety disorder. The reward system in the brain is built to encourage us to approach the identified reward, and the threat system in the brain is built to drive us to avoid the identified threat. As food has been misidentified as a threat, then "go low and slow" for recovery doesn't offer enough exposure to the threat to allow for the threat identification system to eventually stand down. Both patients and practitioners assume that by getting used to incremental increases over time that the process of recovery can be more comfortable. Instead, this approach continues to reinforce avoidance, thus strengthening the cycle of see food, avoid food. The tomorrow where you intend to try that much-feared food, or increase that intake just a bit more, never arrives.

The Homeodynamic Recovery Method incorporates clinical trial data that demonstrates the treatment modality of exposure and response prevention (ERP), originally designed in the treatment of anxiety disorders (specifically phobias), is also suitable for eating disorder treatment as well.[9,10,11]

Drs. Joanna Steinglass and Sarah Parker, researchers investigating the application of ERP therapy for treatment of both AN and BN patients, noted that the anxiety underpinnings, if not addressed, predispose a patient to relapse:

Anxiety has long been noted as a prominent feature of AN, and a high rate of comorbidity between AN and anxiety disorders has frequently been reported. Though generalized anxiety improves as weight is restored, it does not necessarily normalize. Instead, most AN patients continue to show significant psychopathology after successful weight restoration, including abnormal eating behavior, over-concern with weight, and fear of fat.

Individuals who have shown improvement in many psychological symptoms still significantly restrict their eating when observed in a laboratory situation. Furthermore, restrictive eating patterns consisting of a monotonous low-energy, low-density diet have been shown to predict relapse. These restrictive eating patterns may be driven by underlying fear and avoidance of foods, along with fear of certain eating situations, which may in turn be the manifestation of underlying traits of high anxiety and high obsessionality.[12]

Keeping in mind that the brain is impaired due to the absence of energy required to keep it running smoothly, and it's also caught in a threat identification system that ratchets to ever-increasing levels of strength as each avoidance maneuver is enacted and reinforced; there will never be a right time, enough information, or enough iron-clad assurances that will make re-feeding feel like a good choice or a sensible path forward.

You must rely on instinct. You will inherently know if this is the thing you must do, even when you don't want to do it. But before you squeeze your eyes shut and just begin, we have to talk about medical risk. Understand that, on very rare occasions, the shedding wizard may not survive the restoration project.

Re-feeding syndrome

Dr. Laleeq Khan and colleagues provide a thorough systematic review of scientific literature that assessed the medical challenges of re-feeding after a period of starvation. The suite of symptoms is referred to as re-feeding syndrome and was first documented in the 1950s in malnourished prisoners of war:

RFS [re-feeding syndrome] is well recognised. It occurs after the reintroduction of feeding after a period of starvation or fasting. RFS describes a series of metabolic and biochemical changes that occur as a consequence of reintroduction of feeding after a period of starvation or fasting. This unfavorable metabolic response causes nonimmune -mediated harm to the body and can be mild, moderate, or severe.[13]

In re-feeding, after a period of malnourishment, the body has to accommodate to a nutritional load that it has adapted to being without. The symptoms of that response include fluid and electrolyte imbalances with the most common (but not universal) imbalance being hypophosphatemia (low phosphate levels).[14]

In one study, moderate hypophosphatemia occurred in 5.8% of eating disorder patients hospitalized for initial re-feeding. Mild hypophosphatemia with no other complications developed in 21.7% of these patients and it was resolved with supplementation. Patients with moderate hypophosphatemia were more malnourished at the outset.[15]

Despite the fact that the underlying reasons for the condition and the treatment to resolve it are well understood, the circumstances in which RFS are likely to occur and, most importantly, the actual incidence and prevalence rates for those re-feeding from eating disorders, are absent from the research literature at present. As such, we have to go with an amalgamation of case reports where the details are sufficient to enable us to perhaps develop suitable guidelines for risk factors associated with RFS.

Body weights of BMI 19.9 or lower were involved in cases with RFS; however, one case involved a BMI of 35.2. The median BMI was 13.7. The onset of RFS occurred between 0.4 to 21 days with the median being 3 days. Of those who developed RFS, the mortality was 25%, with case reports dating back earlier in time (1940s) having higher mortality than those in more recent times.[16] Problematically, this data incorporates only 49 cases in the literature review—that's very little to go on for developing risk assessment guidelines.

Electrolyte imbalances are a known outcome for those who purge or abuse diuretics and laxatives and yet these eating disorder patients are often average or above-average weight. The abrupt cessation of those maladaptive habits can cause heart and blood vessel damage.[17]

While abrupt cessation of these behaviors is warranted, modest (but necessary) medical intervention will be required to support the body's shift to an absence of purging and/or diuretic or laxative use.

We are all used to advisories to consult our doctor before we so much as comb our hair, but when it comes to a state of malnutrition[†] the advisory to consult your doctor before you begin re-feeding is a non-negotiable statement of urgency.

Incrementing food intake slowly does not necessarily reduce the chance of RFS—that is especially the case for patients with more enduring anorexia or those with few remaining physiological reserves (i.e., extremely low weight, other medical complications already present due to ongoing starvation, etc.).[18]

Unfortunately symptoms of the possible progression of electrolyte imbalances toward full-blown RFS (leading to organ failure in the absence of immediate medical intervention) are also vague. It is wise to err very much on the side of caution within the first 21 days of incrementing food intake upward (usually by increasing 200 calories every other day until at 2000 kcal/day and then jump to the Homeodynamic Recovery Method intake guidelines from there). If you have symptoms of muscle weakness, seizures, dizziness, nausea, vomiting, and feel as if you are coming down with a really bad flu, then visit an emergency department immediately.[19] Be closely monitored by medical professionals while you increase your intake amounts.

---

† Please note that malnutrition is not a state that is purely developed through restriction of food intake. If you have been applying a lot of exercise with insufficient rest and food intake, or if you have been purging or using laxatives and diuretics, then these warnings apply.

Specific deficiencies worth investigation

Supplementation of a diet necessarily means that the diet itself cannot be inadequate for overall energy needs. In other words, if you are actively restricting your food intake then you are not meeting your body's basic energy requirements. A vitamin or mineral supplement is designed to *supplement* (add to) an existing energy-balanced level of food intake. Many with eating disorders lean toward using supplements as meal replacements and these supplements are not designed to replace meals.

Additionally, using supplements when there is no deficiency is at best wasteful and at worst could be dangerous to your health. First and foremost, confirm whether you have a vitamin or mineral deficiency with your doctor before you use supplements during your re-feeding efforts. Consider discussing with your medical practitioner screening for possible deficiencies in zinc,[20,21] magnesium[22,23] and/or thiamine (vitamin B1)[24,25] in advance of entering your recovery efforts. When deficiencies are correctly identified and then supplemented as you re-feed, it can lower the risk of serious complications during re-feeding as well as often ease many of the unpleasant symptoms that occur early in the recovery process.

Zinc, magnesium, and thiamine are by no means the only important minerals and vitamins that might require supplementation during early re-feeding, but they are the most likely deficiencies found in a reasonable minority of those undergoing re-feeding. However, using zinc, magnesium, or thiamine supplements in the absence of a confirmed deficiency could be dangerous in recovery, so play it safe and see your doctor first.

Other medical risks

Clinical levels of restrictive eating are defined as 1000 kcal/day or less. Subclinical levels of restrictive eating are set between >1000 kcal/day up to the total energy requirements as defined for the individual. Now of course those cutoffs are variable, depending on energy expenditure, sex, and age. For example, one comparative study identified subclinical eating disorder intake at 1989 kcal/day for female athletes.[26] Another study identified subclinical restrictive eating as 19% fewer calories along with higher than average Eating Disorder Inventory (EDI) scores compared to healthy controls.[27] Keep in mind that these cutoffs reflect net deficits. If you eat 1600 kcal/day (subclinical restrictive eating) but then are also a distance runner, your net energy deficit will actually result in you having clinical restrictive behaviors because you expend more than 600 calories during the exertion of your daily run (net ≥1000 kcal/day deficit).

The difference between clinical and subclinical levels of restriction is the angle of the grade of deterioration in your health.

An adult woman (biologically speaking, that would be women at or over the age of 25 [28]) with subclinical restrictive eating could be consuming a maximum of 2025 kcal/day (or 19% of confirmed average intake of 2500 kcal/day for healthy controls).‡

There is no clear understanding within the practitioner or research communities as to whether activation of the eating disorder spectrum can really appear for the first time in a mature adult, or

---

‡ Please see doubly-labeled water method trial data following on in this chapter for clinical data confirming that the recommended daily calorie intake of 2000 kilocalories for women is incorrect and invalid.

whether it was activated in child or adolescent years but maintained a subclinical presence until later life. Dr. Kathryn Zerbe, MD, psychiatrist and clinical professor at Oregon Health and Sciences University, wrote a short article on the current understanding of eating disorders that appear in mature adults within the psychiatric and medical communities:

> In the 1980s, examples of "late life eating disorders" in the literature were intriguing but rare, and for the most part a biological explanation was given for their etiology and resistance to intervention. In the 21st Century, clinicians see more patients who have maintained full-blown or subclinical eating and body image problems for decades... No matter the cause, eating disorders in the older population are dangerous illnesses that beguile practitioners who must be alert to the myriad of medical "rule outs" that must be made before the diagnosis of eating disorder is given.[29]

Subclinical restrictive eating behaviors manifest negative health impacts over decades, whereas clinical restrictive eating behaviors manifest negative health impacts over mere months or years. Remembering that restrictive eating behaviors are cumulative in their impacts on the body, many patients who are diagnosed with late-onset eating disorders have actually experienced a long-running subclinical condition that has met the threshold for clinical diagnosis in later life just because the medical complications are compounding due to years of cumulative damage.

One of the main reasons that the dangerous illnesses caused by ongoing restrictive eating behaviors in older adult patients "beguile" medical practitioners is that patients fail to divulge their long history of such behaviors. In many cases, they are not even aware that their behaviors constitute the presence of an eating disorder. And unfortunately, even if they are forthcoming, often physicians are not as aware as Dr. Kathryn Zerbe (quoted above) that such behaviors are indeed responsible for numerous and often seemingly unrelated serious medical illnesses:

1. Moderate to severe osteoporosis

2. Kidney, liver, heart damage

3. Likely both clinical depression and/or anxiety—intractable and progressively unresponsive to treatment

4. Sexual dysfunction due to organ atrophy and low reproductive hormone levels

5. Digestive tract issues: constipation, malabsorption, gastroesophageal reflux disease, multiple intolerances due to insufficiency of digestive enzymes, gastroparesis, etc.

6. Anemia

7. Susceptibility to serious complications with infection

8. Damage to key areas of the brain that manage memory and retention, possibly leading to early-onset dementia

9. A reduced life expectancy of 12 years (approximately)

10. Usually disabled from work when the patient reaches mid to late 40s

11. Severely reduced quality of life requiring on average six or more prescriptions to remediate various painful and debilitating symptoms in the patient's 40s and 50s.

If you pursue a recovery effort after a decade or more of subclinical restrictive eating behaviors, then just as with those who are attempting the process after many months or a few years of clinical restrictive eating behaviors, there is still cumulative latent damage present.

All patients undertaking recovery from an undernourished state are moving a brittle living system into a new state of resiliency. That process stresses a fragile system.

The vast majority will experience unpleasant but essentially benign and temporary symptoms: exhaustion, swelling, pain, etc. For further details on those symptoms, it's best to review the papers and posts on The Eating Disorder Institute website. The symptoms are not due to re-feeding and resting, but rather the body's process of healing the damage that accrued during the active eating disorder period.

For a very small minority, the body has underlying damage that will be exacerbated by the recovery effort. In those circumstances, medical intervention is a necessity. Beyond the very rare instances of RFS, the heart, gastrointestinal organs, and kidneys are most vulnerable to serious medical emergencies (again in those rare cases where underlying damage is severe due to prior restriction).

Unfortunately hyper-intervention is the common framework applied by the medical community today—the result of mounting fears regarding medical malpractice and ever-more questionable application of standards of care developed by administrative specialists within medical and hospital corporations that remove the individual physician's autonomy and expertise from the diagnosis and treatment options. I will address how a patient might navigate these challenges, while undergoing a recovery effort, in the following chapter.

It is important to have an engaged physician for whom both the risk of life threatening complications and iatrogenic complications (i.e., illness or damage exclusively caused by medical intervention) are kept front of mind.

Common misdiagnoses either prior to or during recovery

Many patients with active eating disorders will be diagnosed with hypothyroidism or autoimmune hypothyroidism (Hashimoto's thyroiditis).

Given that Hashimoto's thyroiditis has a prevalence of 2 in 100,[30] the rate at which I see this condition diagnosed in those with eating disorders who are of average or above-average weight at the time of diagnosis is staggeringly higher than what it should be.

There are many ways in which we can overtreat patients both when they are actively restricting food intake and when they undergo recovery from an eating disorder. Prescribing thyroid replacement hormone is one of the most common ways in which we interfere too quickly in a process that is most likely going to resolve with absolutely no intervention, given time and continued re-feeding and rest.

The prescribing of thyroid hormone treatment has increased approximately 30% in the UK in the past 10 years.[31] That is largely due to new lower cutoff points for the classification of hypothyroidism, even though there is no good data to confirm that treating patients at these cutoff points yields measurable long-term benefit. Instances of autoimmune hypothyroidism overdiagnosis may also be due to transient repair of the thyroid misdiagnosed as antibody-generated pathology.[32]

In other words, misdiagnosis is quite possible for those with a history of an eating disorder. Almost all physicians and endocrinologists overlook the fact that a hypothyroid state is often entirely resolvable were the patient merely encouraged to reverse the energy deficit within her body.

There is insufficient clinical data to confirm whether restrictive eating behaviors activate autoimmune hypothyroidism; however, a parallel circumstance seen in postpartum women may indicate that the presence of autoimmune hypothyroidism in patients with an eating disorder is not, in fact, Hashimoto's thyroiditis.

Postpartum patients can develop transient autoimmune hypothyroiditis, suggesting that dropping reproductive hormone levels have something to do with the activation of this transient state. Resolution of transient autoimmune hypothyroiditis likely coincides with reproductive hormone levels returning to their optimal state.[33] Given that patients who restrict food take the boots to their reproductive hormone levels, then it's possible that there are transient autoantibodies present due to fluctuating reproductive hormone levels and that these autoantibodies are not destroying thyroid tissue just as is the case with postpartum autoimmune hypothyroiditis as well. As such, no treatment intervention would be required beyond resting and re-feeding.

As for hypothyroidism that appears in the absence of any antibodies, it is a known outcome of even intermittent fasting, such as is found in subjects adhering to daytime fasting for Ramadan.[§,34] For those with eating disorders, low triiodothyronine (T3) is common, and during re-feeding both T3 and tetraiodothyronine (T4) may drop even further before returning to match healthy control levels after a sustained period of rest and re-feeding.[35]

If your practitioner diagnoses you with hypothyroidism, autoimmune or otherwise, then consider discussing a wait-and-see approach while you pursue your recovery effort. Keep in mind that each patient is different and it will be for you and your doctor to determine together whether your particular results indicate immediate intervention is necessary or not.

Another common misdiagnosis for those with eating disorders is polycystic ovarian syndrome (PCOS). PCOS may include increased facial hair, weight gain, and a lack of a regular menstrual cycle. However, PCOS should not be diagnosed in a patient with a coexisting eating disorder unless and until the patient is in a full remission from the eating disorder.

If a patient were diagnosed with PCOS prior to the onset of an eating disorder, then she would need to have been older than at least 21 at the time of the PCOS diagnosis as prior to that age, immature

§ Please note that the leaders of all religions that include religion-based pursuits of fasting or food restriction are familiar with extending medical dispensation for individual followers. Not only that, they are demonstrably supportive of those who are not able to partake for health reasons and refute all arguments that not partaking is in any way a faithless act.

ovaries can lead to misdiagnosis. Polycystic ovaries are common in maturing females and can also appear transiently in mature females without signifying any syndrome in need of medical intervention.[36,37]

Clinical studies suggest that approximately 50% PCOS diagnoses are incorrect for a variety of reasons. There is both a level of overdiagnosis and lack of reproducibility in the screening and clinical criteria used that suggest that the entire condition is hard to identify and it has many phenotypic variables.

The data suggest that there is considerable uncertainty of all measurements and lack of clarity of the definition of the term "hyperandrogenaemia" which can lead to misdiagnosis. The current diagnostic strategies for PCOS are defined too vaguely to ascertain that individuals fit the definition of the syndrome.[38]

Therefore an "official" PCOS diagnosis should be approached with extreme skepticism.

Polycystic ovaries occur in several circumstances where treatment is not required and, for those who are under-eating relative to their energy requirements, the presence of polycystic ovaries reflects the atrophy of the entire reproductive system as the body's way to keep going despite cumulative energy deficits. Facial hair growth indicates hyperandrogenism. However its presence, in conjunction with the presence of an active eating disorder, often reflects low levels of estradiol and other female reproductive hormone levels *relative* to androgen levels, rather than confirming true elevated levels of androgens.

Such symptoms, when they are the result of an eating disorder, will resolve with rest and re-feeding. Again, many practitioners will assume in error that someone of average or above-average weight cannot have an eating disorder. Many misdiagnosed cases of PCOS are the result of this profound misconception that patients who just "don't look anorexic" cannot have an active eating disorder. It will be up to you to apprise your health care provider of your energy deficit status and to decide to move on if you determine that they are too steeped in cultural fattism to familiarize themselves with the scientific data.

Clinical data is readily available regarding the reproductive and fertility impacts of an eating disorder for women, however there are equivalent reproductive and fertility impacts in men with eating disorders.[39] The same is also true for anyone undergoing any kind of gender reassignment as well.

One further area of misdiagnosis for those with a history of an eating disorder that is not quite as straightforward as hypothyroidism or PCOS in recovery will involve blood glucose issues. Seriously out-of-range blood glucose results can occur in re-feeding and may require medical intervention until your pancreas is receiving enough energy to get back up to speed. A dietician can be very helpful for those dealing with either hypo- or hyperglycemia in early re-feeding to keep the recovery process moving forward safely. Yet again, however, there is a marked prejudice against average- and above average–sized patients when nonthreatening and modest shifts in blood glucose management occur and health practitioners may advise aggressive treatment with, most commonly, use of the drug metformin.

Hypercortisolism (elevated cortisol levels) may also develop for some in recovery and as with blood glucose issues tends to resolve with continued rest and re-feeding. Watchful waiting removes the possibility of unnecessary treatment but it may not always possible to go that route and keep the patient safe at the same time. Make your case for watchful waiting but then listen closely to your doctor's assessment and recommendations when it comes to your unique situation.

Thankfully most physicians will be willing to take a wait-and-see approach if warranted, but they may not always offer it as an option. Asking if it's possible to retest in three months' time often allows for enough time to reveal a trend towards the norm. Waiting to reveal the trend will allow everyone to feel confident that either nature can take its course or perhaps intervention is warranted to support the recovery effort.

Energy depletion is not a BMI

Probably most of you are aware that the clinical marker for active anorexia was body mass index (BMI) 17.5 or less within the DSM-IV. Thankfully this marker has been removed from the DSM-5 in recognition of the fact that the marker is misleading. The so-called healthy BMI range (18.5 to 24.9) cannot reflect health status as the entire BMI scale does not reveal health status. BMI is merely a mathematical equation that allows for us to plot the incidence of weight over height squared across the entire human population. We each have an inherited specific optimal weight and it's the effort of trying to lower our weight in relation to that inherited state that actually impacts health status.

I usually explain it this way:

Imagine there are two women of the same height and one is naturally meant to be BMI 37[¶] and the other is naturally BMI 21. Both decide to diet and exercise as a way to lose weight.

Here is what happens:

The woman at BMI 37 achieves a new BMI level of 30. She is classified as "obese"; receives compliments on her dieting efforts; and is encouraged to "keep going."

The woman at BMI 21 drops 4 points to BMI 17. People are very worried and suggest she needs to stop dieting.

Which one has an active eating disorder? They both do. Furthermore, the woman who is being encouraged to lose further weight has commensurately more physiological damage than the woman who is being encouraged to eat more. Both need intervention to recover and yet only one will be identified as needing treatment.

For many who experience cycles of restricting food intake combined with instances of reactively eating, the body responds to that stress by increasing the size of the fat organ to try to modulate the negative impacts of cycles of energy depletion on the body's metabolic functions.[40] A patient with an inherited optimal weight set point of BMI 26 might find herself at BMI 30 after 10 years of trying to restrict and her body fighting back with bouts of reactive eating.[41,42,43,44,45]

¶ As a reminder, standard deviation from the mean for weight allows for plenty of individuals in our society to have inherited a natural optimal weight set point of BMI 30 and above (see previous chapter for further details).

No matter your current BMI, choosing to apply the Homeodynamic Recovery Method is based on your determination of whether restrictive eating behaviors are harming your quality of life or not.

Many patients worry that, because they are already restoring weight on less than minimum intake calorie amounts, they will "over" restore or gain more "than needed" if they further increase their intake. However, weight restoration is not linear to intake amount increases. Much of the energy needed in recovery is used to repair of damage and restore suppressed or dormant biological functions within the body. The body restores weight first to insulate vital organs. Weight, body mass indices, body fat percentages as well as mass and shape are never markers of the body's energy status or health.

The minimum calorie needs outlined within the Homeodynamic Recovery Method are applicable to non–eating disorder equivalents, based on doubly labeled water trial method confirmation. This methodology measures calorie intake and energy expenditure and is utterly accurate.**,[46],[47]

** The use of doubly labeled water to assess free-living energy expenditure has a reported precision of ±3% and is also used to validate other methods used to measure energy expenditure. Doubly labeled water is noninvasive and involves ingesting water labeled with a known concentration of naturally occurring, stable isotopes of hydrogen and oxygen. As energy is expended in the body, carbon dioxide and water are produced, and the differences between the isotope elimination rates are used to calculate total energy expenditure.

Calorie needs for everyone else

We lie about what we eat. Yes, in health survey after health survey, adult women report eating on average just under 2000 kcal/day and men around 2500 kcal/day.[48,49,50] Yet when we actually measure the intake and expenditure in laboratory settings rather than relying on self-generated food journals or survey responses, then subjects eat about one-quarter to one-third more than the surveys would suggest they are eating.

Dr. Dale Schoeller, a professor emeritus with the department of nutritional sciences at the Institute on Aging, University of Wisconsin, specializes in the area of physical activity and obesity, and he has this to say on the validity of doubly labeled water method when compared to our traditional dependence on self-reports for determining energy needs in human beings:

The measurement of dietary intake by self-report has played a central role in nutritional science for decades... Recently, the doubly-labeled water method has been validated for the measurement of total energy expenditure in free-living subjects, and this method can serve as a reference for validating the accuracy of self-reported energy intake. Such comparisons have been made in nine recent studies, and considerable inaccuracy in self-reports of energy intake has been documented. Reported intakes tend to be lower than expenditure and thus are often underestimates of true habitual energy intake. Because the degree of underreporting increases with intake, **it is speculated that individuals tend to report intakes that are closer to perceived norms than to actual intake.**[51] *[emphasis mine]*

Dr. James Hébert, professor at the University of South Carolina, and his colleagues specifically investigated how social desirability and approval might impact reporting errors on food frequency questionnaires, seven-day dietary recall and seven 24-hour dietary recall interviews:

> *Social desirability and social approval distort energy intake estimates from structured questionnaires, in a manner that appears to vary by educational status. For college-educated women with an average social desirability score (~ 17 points) this would equal an underestimate of 507 kcal/day.*[52]

Both 7-day and 14-day self-report trials are all over the map in the actual underreporting that occurs and many researchers will classify trial subjects as failed dieters, obese, average-weighted, etc., which likely removes validity from the trial data, as an inherent bias stands that obese individuals are more prone to underreport food intake—a bias that does not stand up in clinical trial scrutiny.[53] And that bias fails to address other valid influences such as social desirability and approval that are strong motivators for the underreporting of food intake, as highlighted by Dr. Hebert and colleagues (quoted above).

The underreporting for both men and women can range from 2% to 58%. However, in the one and only doubly labeled water trial where two groups of women were identified as either non-restrictors or restrictors of food intake, and all were weight stable, the non-restricting group ate on average 2400 kcal/day and the restricting group ate just shy of 2000 kcal/day.[54] Admittedly this is a small study, but I use it because it identifies a clear non-dieting control group.

If we average the studies reviewed by Dr. Hebert and his colleagues, then people eat on average 25% more than they think they do (or report that they do). As most adult women say they eat just shy of 2000 kcal/day, then on average they actually eat 2500 kcal/day to maintain their health and weight.

But the fact that we eat much more than we say we do does not have any correlation to obesity. It only demonstrates the fact that our actual intakes match our energy expenditures. Doubly labeled water trials are measuring actual energy expenditure. A non-dieting subject, regardless of BMI, will naturally match her energy intake to her energy expenditure.

As a common research bias, we end up knowing more about male energy requirements under all manner of situations when compared to female energy requirements. We know that an 11-man sailing crew traveling around the world averaged 4700 kcal/day; six mountain climbers ascending above 19,000 ft. (6000 m) also required 4700 kcal/day; a short-term space flight equaled similar average intake as found on Earth (2800 kcal/day); soldiers in Zimbabwe required 5600 kcal/day; and yet more soldiers on field operations in extreme cold and heat required 4300 and 3900 kcal/day.[55] As a complete mind bender, consider the fact that the astronauts were eating 2800 kcal/day and they all weighed 0 lbs. (0 kg)—in space you are weightless.

There is one trial that did include female cross-country skiers along with their male counterparts. The energy requirements for the female skiers were 3585 to 4827 kcal/day.[56]

Urban Chinese adult women (age ranges 35–49) had energy intake levels confirmed at 2300 kcal/day. That their intake was somewhat lower than averages found in North America is not due to racial differences but rather a discrepancy in average height (lower in China for that age range).[57] Pregnant adult women require on average 2854 kcal/day in the first trimester, 3070 kcal/day in the second trimester, and 3092 kcal/day in the final trimester.[58]

The compilation of 22 studies indicates that adult women have an average confirmed intake of 2500 kcal/day, using the doubly labeled water method. The average confirmed intake for the adult men was 3400 kcal/day. However, the age range in this compilation for the females was 25 and older, whereas for the males it was 22 and older. Because males younger than 25 will consume more (for developmental reasons), the average intake reported is a bit higher than what is needed for fully matured male adults (approximately 3000 kcal/day).[59]

And all of this data is for those over the age of 25. What does that mean for those between the ages of 12 and 24? One lone doubly labeled water trial confirms that 14-year-old males and females appear to have energy intake requirements that average out at 3072 kcal/day.[60]

In the absence of actual data, we have to use studies of under-reporting on this age group to extract likely energy intake requirements. Worth noting is that in an additional analysis of a representative cross-section of those who completed the French Étude Individuelle Nationale des Consommations Alimentaires dietary survey, 40% of the children ages 11 to 17 had attempted to lose weight in the past year and 41% wanted to weigh less, out of a total of 881 males and females assessed. In the same study, children ages 3 to 10 underreported food intake by 4.8%, and those between ages 11 to 17 underreported by 26%. No significant differences were found between males and females in underreporting values, and no incidences of overreporting occurred for those aged 11 to 17.[61]

In one UK study where the survey results of 16- to 17-year-old female dieters and non-dieters were compared, self-reported intake for dieters was 1604 kcal/day and 2460 kcal/day for non-dieters.[62] Given that underreporting appears to occur at the same rate for 11- to 17-year-olds as it does for their adult counterparts, we can extrapolate that non-dieting teenage girls actually eat 3075 kcal/day to support all their metabolic and developmental needs to arrive at biological adulthood at age 25.

Rather conveniently, 16- to 17-year-old dieting and non-dieting males were also assessed for their self-reported intakes, and male dieters stated they consumed 2190 kcal/day whereas non-dieters stated they consumed 3066 kcal/day.[63] As we know there are no distinctions between rates of underreporting for males and females in this age group, 16- to 17-year-old non-dieting males actually eat 3833 kcal/day to support development to age 25.

And there you have it: **none of the above solid data on actual required energy intake for various age and sex-matched subgroups applies to you if you have an eating disorder. This data applies only to energy-*balanced* individuals; and those with eating disorders are energy *deficient*.**

Homeodynamic Recovery Method food intake guidelines

The Homeodynamic Recovery Method minimum intake guidelines are age-, height-, and sex-matched based on energy intake requirements for equivalent healthy controls. They are based on all the amassed hard data listed above. Of course this is confusing as I have just stated that these intake levels are for energy-balanced individuals and when you have an eating disorder, you are energy depleted. The reason the minimum intakes are set to these levels is that it is a reasonable way to get you started. You will need more than minimum intake to reach remission (see section "Hyperphagia" below).

Adult female

You are a 25+ year-old female between 5'0" and 5'8" (152 to 173 cm): **minimum 2500 kcal/day**.

Adult male

You are a 25+ year-old male between 5'4" and 6'0" (163 to 183 cm): **minimum 3000 kcal/day**.

Adolescent female

You are an under 25-year-old female between 5'0" and 5'8" (152 to 173 cm): **minimum 3000 kcal/day**.

Adolescent male

You are an under 25-year-old male between 5'4" and 6'0" (162 to 183 cm): **minimum 3500 kcal/day**.

Outside the height ranges listed above

If you are taller than the height guidelines listed above, then expect to add approximately 200 kcal/day to the minimum intake amounts listed for your shorter counterparts (age and sex matched).

If you are shorter than the height guidelines listed above, then you may eat 200 kcal/day less than the minimum intake listed for your taller age and sex matched counterparts; however, keep in mind that these are average intake guidelines for those without an eating disorder—you should find yourself wanting to eat far more than these intake guidelines during your recovery process as hyperphagia will kick in to help you replenish the energy deficit in the body.

Outside the assumed weight ranges

The intake values are confirmed averages for those of average height and weight. The vast majority of the population is of average height and of average weight—almost all of us are sitting on or near that peak of the bell-shaped curve. The absolute peak is BMI 27ish, with the range in which approximately 70% of the population will reside at BMI 21 to 30.[64]

Only 4% of the adult population is naturally meant to be between BMI 18.5 to 20.9. There is a steep slope up from the x-axis to the peak of the bell curve on the left-hand size and a shallow slope down from the peak of the curve to the x-axis on the right-hand side. Human beings cannot survive being exceedingly tall or exceedingly thin as well as they can survive being exceedingly short or exceedingly fat (see Figure 1 [65]).

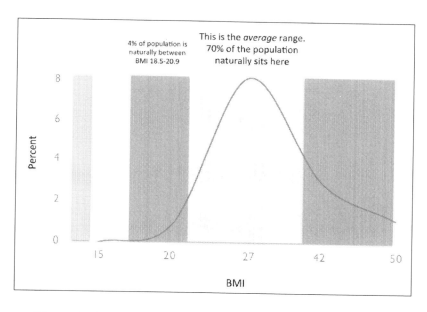

Figure 1. Average BMI range

During the re-feeding phase of recovery, no matter your current BMI, use your age-, sex-, current weight- and height-matched minimum intake amounts and respond fully to the extreme hunger that will likely occur (as per the re-feeding experience for those who were part of the Minnesota Starvation Experiment). If you share an inherited optimal weight set point with the 26% of our population who is naturally above BMI 30, then your daily intake requirements will be higher than average as well. Expect to add an additional 200 to 300 calories to create your daily minimum intake in recovery if you are between BMI 30 and 48.

I realize that this concept will be absolutely horrifying to most people, but as Drs. Philip Mehler and Arnold Anderson pointed out: *"someone has to hold down the upper standard deviation from the average, although few women accept this fact..."* [66] And as we saw in the Étude Individuelle Nationale des Consommations Alimentaires mentioned in a previous section, both boys and girls between ages 11 and 17 are equally under reporting food intake, suggesting that social acceptability of weight impacts both sexes today.

Parents of young children and / or unavoidable work-based activity

Resting is a critical component of the recovery process, so it is understood that no discretionary activity will be undertaken during recovery: no exercise and workouts.

However much it might be ideal for a patient to convalesce fully during the recovery process, both financial and familial obligations mean that many patients have to face unavoidable activity. In these cases, patients should consider assigning themselves a minimum intake that is 500–1000 kcal more than the intake assigned for their age and sex. But it is very important to recognize that it is not a linear equation in that physical activity is not fully compensated during recovery merely by upping food intake. We know that an energy-depleted body makes conservative metabolic choices that can lead to weight gain in the presence of ongoing energy intake deficits.[67] We also know that women with restriction-induced functional hypothalamic amenorrhea (absence of a regular menstrual cycle due to energy depletion in the body) are rarely able to restore menstruation with increased food intake alone, and they must also stop athletic endeavors at the same time to be successful.[68]

When your financial means depend upon a job where you are active (standing, walking or something with significant exertion), consider some of these possible options that other patients have used to try to help their recovery efforts:

1. Coincide the first few weeks of recovery with using up your holiday allotment (if you have that privilege).

2. Seek a doctor's note for sick leave for the initial six weeks where the worst of the exhaustion tends to hit.

3. Investigate any possibility of a temporary work-share with another employee to drop your hours (if you can take the financial hit).

Many patients I have interacted with are unable to entertain the above options and in those cases remission might still be achieved by unabashedly transferring all nonessential activity to loved ones (family and/or friends). Such activities will include household cleaning, general chores and errands, and anything that does not pertain to income-based obligations.

For parents who are primary caregivers (i.e., not an income-based obligation, but most certainly an obligatory effort), make every attempt to transfer as much of the caregiving duties as possible and shift responsibilities elsewhere to ensure sleep duration and quality are improved as much as is feasible.

Try to keep in mind that the ability you have now to place your recovery effort first will greatly enhance your ability to continue to earn a living over the long term as well as to give you the opportunity to be there for your children as they grow.

You will be tempted to classify many things as "unavoidable activity" because you are compelled to do so as part of an active eating disorder. So involve a family member, trusted friend, or therapist in helping you push back on what you might deem unavoidable when compared to what someone who doesn't deal with an eating disorder might deem unavoidable.

A note on counting calories

Someone with an active eating disorder cannot "eat intuitively" or depend on hunger cues to provide sufficient energy to the body. Anxiety responses create a strong and constant pressure to avoid food. As such, a patient should ensure she eats the minimum intake guidelines within each 24-hour period.

However, counting calories can be anxiety provoking in itself and lead to obsessive compulsivity associated with weighing and measuring food portions. In those cases, patients should involve a dietician or nutritionist to help develop a meal plan. The meal plan should be designed to meet *and exceed* the minimum intake guidelines. The patient can then focus her attention on merely ticking off the items on the daily intake list, thereby minimizing the anxiety of counting calories for each food item.

It is just fine to ask a family member or friend for help in designing the meal plan as well. Whether it is a meal plan or a calorie-counting exercise, the goal is to relinquish all control to hunger and accept the onslaught of extreme hunger.

Many patients are keen to move to "intuitive eating" very early in the process of recovery. Resist the urge to do so until well beyond phase two; otherwise relapse can occur.

Hyperphagia in recovery

August 2, 2012 - Kimberly

Not too long ago, I put some hash browns in the oven and decided to have some toast while I waited. While the toast was in the toaster, I had some cashews and poured myself a bowl of yoghurt—so, essentially, I was having a snack while I waited for the second snack that I was preparing while I waited for the first snack. SNACKCEPTION.

You'll recall that we looked at the hyperphagia (extreme eating) that occurred for the subjects in the Minnesota Starvation Experiment in chapter 3. Patients find extreme hunger very upsetting and disturbing in recovery, so I will examine this in some detail before moving onto the phases of recovery as a whole. So pervasive are the misconceptions regarding binge eating and so-called emotional eating as dangerous and unacceptable behaviors that lead to ill health and obesity, it takes herculean focus to maintain respectful responsiveness to the demands for energy that the body is making.

In simplified terms, several hormones including leptin and adiponectin can activate adenosine monophosphate-activated protein kinase (AMPK) and that in turn regulates metabolic choices between anabolism (resulting in the building up of tissue) and catabolism (resulting in the breaking down of tissue).[69] These same hormones also act on the brain and specifically interact with the hypothalamus, which is responsible for identifying whether energy balance is present or absent throughout the entire body. Leptin and adiponectin, as well as resistin and several others, are all generated by cells within the fat organ of your body.[70]

In our current understanding of the cycle of these adipocytokines (as these fat-generated hormones are called as a group), their serum levels are affected by restriction of energy intake (even before catabolism occurs); they "inform" the hypothalamus of an energy deficit; *and* they activate AMPK to begin the process of catabolism of existing body tissue (made up of cells, obviously) to release energy to support ongoing biological functions.

One of the reasons that those with an active eating disorder often do not appear deficient in many minerals and vitamins may not actually be due to their heavy use of vitamin and mineral supplements, but rather the release of these minerals and vitamins through catabolism of their own body tissue.[71] Catabolism (the destruction of cells and tissue) releases the energy necessary to try to remediate the drop in serum adipocytokine levels while at the same time those levels are signaling the hypothalamus that energy intake is a necessity to reverse the process of catabolism.

When you see the word "catabolism," think cannibalization of your own being.

It is rather obvious to point out that, in the aftermath of restriction, the catabolism (breakdown of tissue) has to be reversed with anabolism (the buildup of tissue). Nonetheless, this process is complicated further as the gastrointestinal tract has its own nervous system—the enteric nervous system—and specific peptide hormones are released by the gastrointestinal tract in response to the presence of food as well: peptide YY, pancreatic polypeptide, glucagon-like peptide-1, and oxyntomodulin. And these peptides are all presumed to act as postprandial satiety (after-a-meal fullness) signals.[72]

Your gut and your mind

When a person is energy balanced, then hunger, fullness, and satiation are all synchronized. But after just a few weeks (let alone months or years) of catabolizing your own body, these things will be asynchronous when you begin to reverse the damage.

In the earlier phases of recovery, you experience significant sensory dissonance because physical fullness, as identified by your enteric nervous system, and extreme absence of satiation, as experienced by your central nervous system are confirming you are both full and hungry at the same time.

Here are several first-person accounts of what it actually feels like from The Eating Disorder Institute members posting on the forums:

"The concept to me is so confusing, because I can feel not hungry, satiated, or even nauseous with food, but there isn't necessarily fullness in my stomach."

"I have only been hitting my minimums consistently for a week and am now beginning (from two days ago) to get extreme hunger. It's such an odd sensation of never feeling full and constantly just wanting to eat food then feeling absolutely stuffed...I just hate extreme hunger to be honest, and I wish I could just happily walk through recovery hitting my minimums. I guess this isn't realistic for the amount of damage our bodies have undertaken, though, is it."

"I definitely feel some compulsion to "finish everything" now, because I fear being deprived and am still obsessed with food to varying degrees. I am also very, very aware of my hunger. It's weird that I seriously cannot remember how I ate before I started restricting..."

"I think I feel the food in my stomach, and I definitely feel "full", but I still feel the urge to "finish everything", too. Sometimes I feel like I am just forcing the food down. I don't know whether it's a lack of fullness or satiation, but I can definitely relate to never feeling full."

"Even then if there was still food on my plate I would almost force myself to finish it because it "tasted so good". I am really not sure what this is or what it means...if I was not full to bursting I would still feel hungry/not satiated."

"I've recently (within a week or two) started to experience extreme hunger. It is nerve-racking: I feel some sort of hunger or emptiness in my stomach while also being full and bloated and feeling nauseous at the thought of food at the same time. It is truly bizarre and I sometimes hear myself say "oh god, please I don't want to eat anymore" but the hunger persists and I force another sandwich down my throat."

For these patients, the brain structures responsible for conscious thought are dealing with a completely novel experience, and it's easy to see the profound struggle that it elicits. Biologically speaking, they are all gut-full yet brain-empty.

And the above quotes confirm there is tremendous variation in how those sensory contradictions are awkwardly resolved with post-hoc rationalization. One feels fullness in the stomach but no sense of satiation, and yet the next person will describe exactly opposite sensations.

Your enteric nervous system is receiving information that the physical aspects of energy absorption are at peak levels, yet the central nervous system continues to receive information that more anabolism (building up of tissue) is required to return to an energy-balanced state.

Try not to get too caught up in what descriptions your conscious mind generates to try to make sense of the nonsensical as you move through these phases of recovery. Your job is to eat. The anxieties about whether it is "normal," "emotional," or "the stomach has adapted to more food" are just that: anxieties.

If you feel the need to eat more, then it doesn't matter how your mind describes that need; the drive to eat is fundamentally sound and all about energy restoration, or anabolism.

Three-legged stool for success

As touched on in the previous chapter, the Homeodynamic Recovery Method for attempting to achieve remission from an eating disorder is built upon a sturdy three-legged stool where each leg is described as follows:

1. Weight restoration (re-feeding)

2. Repair of physical damage (resting)

3. Developing new non-restrictive neural patterns in response to usual anxiety triggers (brain re-training)

An easier way to remember the method is as the three "R"s to remission: re-feeding, resting, and re-training.

It is best to develop your three-legged stool toward remission by attending to the above facets in order. However, you cannot sit on a two-legged stool, so the sooner you are consuming the minimum intake, the sooner you will have enough energy for the brain to be able to handle the work you will undertake (with a suitable counselor or therapist) to develop the new non-restrictive neural patterns. Remember to involve your medical advisor *before* you begin upping calorie intake.

Phases of recovery

The Homeodynamic Recovery Method comprises four phases toward remission of an eating disorder: initial re-feeding, the neither/nor phase, the must-be-done-by-now phase, and the high-risk final phase.

Initial re-feeding

The "weight" gain in the first few days, once you are at minimum intake guidelines for your age, sex and height, is drastic. It can range from 7–16 lbs. (3.1–7.5 kg) in a matter of days. For those observed within hospital settings, the "weight" increase can be upward of 30 lbs. (13.6 kg) within the first two weeks (at full re-feeding intake amounts). The reason that "weight" appears in quotation marks is that the initial drastic increase is primarily due to both extracellular and intracellular water gain.[73,74] Both extracellular and intracellular edema (water retention) occur for two distinct reasons at once in the early phase of recovery: reversible damage to kidney function and macrophage functions for cellular repair throughout the body.

There is diminished creatinine clearance and impaired osmoregulation present for most patients with a history of eating disorders—the kidneys are basically not quite up for the job of healthy water regulation within the body.[75,76] The kidneys recover with continued re-feeding for the vast majority of patients.

Swelling (edema) is also a fundamental body defense to protect the body from further damage or infection and to facilitate healing. The process of healing involves natural cell death (apoptosis); reabsorption and excretion; cell growth and division; and cell differentiation and movement. Macrophages are a dedicated cell type responsible for chomping up damaged cells, triggering fluid ingress and retention, and producing insulin-like-growth-factor-1 to speed up cellular growth and division.[77] The side effects of their presence in our bodies are, of course, swelling and pain.

However the absence of macrophages will result in an equivalent absence of restoration and healing. It is important in this early phase of re-feeding to allow yourself to react to the swelling, pain, and exhaustion appropriately: don't attempt to override the natural healing process, and do your utmost to rest as that kind of pain and swelling would dictate you should do.[78]

Drs. Paul Pencharz and Marcia Azcue used bioelectrical impedance to monitor the response to re-feeding for malnourished patients. Many outside the specialty of eating disorders are utterly unfamiliar with the appearance of edema during re-feeding after a period of starvation:

> *Refeeding oedema in patients with anorexia nervosa is a known but yet under-reported and poorly-understood condition.... Refeeding oedema generally resolves spontaneously but some individuals may require treatment.*[79]

Dr. Stefan Ehrlich and his colleagues at the University Hospital Carl Gustav Carus (Clinic for Child and Adolescent Psychiatry and Psychotherapy) have this to say regarding the presence of re-feeding edema:

> *As in our patient, refeeding oedema usually resolves spontaneously... the occurrence of refeeding oedema has critical implications for psychotherapy. Firstly, patients may be in great distress about the sudden and unexpected weight gain. Repeated medical counselling about the transient nature of the oedema and associated weight gain can help the patient cope...*[80]

Stepping on the scales will confirm that gravity is still working against the mass of your body, and there is little value in constantly reaffirming the presence of gravity. More importantly, weighing yourself tends to precipitate relapse for anyone with an eating disorder. Some treatment teams will suggest that you weigh yourself as a way to lower the anxiety regarding your weight. However, this recommendation fails to attend to behaviors in order of their impact on quality of life. You can feasibly avoid weighing yourself with absolutely no negative impact on your quality of life; and that is absolutely not the case if you avoid food. The priority for you and your treatment team should be for you to practice approaching and eating food.

Human beings survived well not knowing their weights for millennia. We have no more need of knowing our weight than our blink rates or VO_2 max.[††] Your priority is to learn to respond to hunger because the structures in your brain that ensure you maintain your optimal weight set point are not cognitively controlled. Your job is to eat and you let the rest of it take care of itself.

Along with the edema, pain, and swelling, you will likely face a fair amount of digestive distress. Essentially there are four main areas of digestive distress: gastroparesis, enteric nervous system damage, gut microbiome dysfunction, and lower than optimal digestive enzyme production.

Gastroparesis is a life-saving maneuver on the part of the gastro-intestinal system to attempt to maximize accessibility of nutrients when a person is starving. Gastroparesis is delayed emptying of the contents of the stomach into the small intestine. Pulverizing and disintegrating the food longer in the stomach increases the chance that more nutrients can be absorbed through the gut lining of the small intestine. For those with eating disorders, gastroparesis

---

†† VO2 max is peak oxygen uptake or maximal aerobic capacity.

can essentially double the time during which food remains in the stomach. In fact motility throughout the entire gastrointestinal tract is slowed to maximize nutrient absorption.[81] Problematically, it makes the person feel very full. For most patients gastroparesis resolves with continued re-feeding in a matter of weeks. Feeding in smaller doses on a more constant basis, using a heating pad (or ice packs if that feels better) around the abdomen, and consuming ultra-processed, calorie-dense, and easily digestible foods can all help to resolve the slowed motility.[82]

Slowed gut motility can also be the result of enteric nerve damage. As Dr. Janice Russell explained in a radio interview, the demyelination of nerves [during restriction] is a process of making up for energy deficits within the body and it's akin to throwing the antique furniture on the fire to keep the house warm.[83]

The reversal of demyelination has been confirmed within the central nervous systems of patients after weight normalization and we have every reason to suspect the same holds true for both the enteric (gut) and peripheral nervous systems as well.[84,85] However, should gastroparesis be present due to nerve damage, then the resolution will take longer than when it is a functional survival effort of slowed motility to enhance nutrient extraction.

The bacteria throughout the gastrointestinal system are critical for digestive and immune function. As with everything else in your body, those friendly bacteria have suffered huge losses thanks to restrictive eating behaviors. The bacterial colonies will be restored with continued re-feeding, but initially their low colony counts due to starvation can mean diarrhea, gas, bloating, poorly digested foods, and also systemic signs that the gut lining is allowing the wrong things through to the bloodstream (skin rashes and itchiness).[86]

Digestive enzymes are also suboptimal and that means you may face challenges digesting some food. Many make the mistake of assuming they have food intolerances because they have unpleasant symptoms eating dairy or wheat products, but these are almost always secondary food intolerances. Secondary food intolerance means that you are not inherently unable to produce the correct digestive enzymes, but rather an underlying medical condition is the cause of the low digestive enzyme production. In this case the medical condition is an eating disorder. Discuss the possibility with your doctor of using digestive enzyme supplements to ease the symptoms when eating the offending macronutrients until your pancreas is back up to speed. Those with primary lactose intolerance will remain intolerant to dairy products, but keep in mind that lactose is not present in most cheeses, and yogurt is usually well tolerated because it has lactase present to help with digestion.

Once the decision is made to re-feed, there may be an initial few weeks of a honeymoon phase. The patient relishes being able to respond fully to hunger and eat all the forbidden and off-limits foods that she has been denied during active restriction. Extreme hunger (discussed in the previous chapter) kicks in for most as soon as they reach the minimum intake guidelines and patients will readily eat 6000–8000+ kcal/day. The honeymoon is short-lived. Soon the anxiety ratchets up and suddenly it starts to get really hard to keep approaching and eating the food.

The honeymoon is not there for everyone of course. Many find it miserable to be sloshing around with massive edema and pain along with really unpleasant gastrointestinal distress throughout the entire day (and night) as well.

But for both camps, I see a much greater reluctance to cease all exertion and exercise than I see an inability to get to, and beyond, the minimum intake guidelines each day. The topic of exercise and exertion as it relates to a recovery effort is too broad, and important, to cover off in this basic guide. Suffice to say that the cessation of all exertion and exercise is critical to reaching remission from an eating disorder.[‡‡]

One final note on this first phase for women: the absence of regular menstruation absolutely denotes that the body is not at its natural optimal weight set point; however the presence of regular menstruation does not confirm the body is at its optimal weight set point. Confusing I know, but menstruation is a one-directional health marker. Yet again, more detail is available at The Eating Disorder Institute in the papers on reproductive health.

Conundrum of pain

Most pain experienced in recovery is not a marker of something going wrong or being wrong. Pain is an integrated part of healing. Pain stops you from moving areas of the body that are damaged thereby avoiding the chance you will cause further damage. Pain forces you to rest.

[‡‡] To understand all the reasons why maintaining exertion and exercise routines are counterproductive to reaching remission, please look at The Eating Disorder Institute website papers on the topic of exercise.

The art of medicine consists of keeping the patient in a good mood while nature does the healing. — Voltaire

Voltaire's observation probably has more truth to it than our current medical industrial complex would be willing to admit. Nonetheless, we have very skewed concepts of what the healing process entails.

Just fire up a new window in your web browser for a moment and type in the word "healing" under Google Images…see what I mean? It's all colors, light, hands, butterflies, beatific expressions…

The reality of healing any living system is pain, swelling, itching, aches, exhaustion and chaos.

For those in recovery there is often narrowing focus on whether the end state will be worth it and whether the reversal of damage will be total, and the real challenge actually lies within the ability, or inability, to abide while the healing process unfolds.

If there is one thing I'd learned about hospitals, it's that they aren't interested in healing you. They are interested in stabilizing you, and then everyone is supposed to move on. They go to stabilize some more people, and you go off to do whatever you do. Healing, if it happens at all, is done on your own, long after the hospital has submitted your final insurance paperwork. — Eric Nuzum

If you are a reader of The Eating Disorder Institute forums, then you are likely well aware of the fact that many people struggle greatly through the process of healing. Some have even had full-blown medical crises: pancreatitis, diabetic attacks, worsening of preexisting conditions (eczema, allergic reaction, digestive distress, inflammatory responses of one kind or another) and one or two have even faced re-feeding syndrome.

Many speak of their frustration with the symptoms that plague them throughout recovery that were completely absent when they were actively restricting energy intake.

We tend to acclimatize to progressive worsening of active conditions, but find it shocking when crises occur when we are actively pursuing healing.

We expect the healing process to be full of color, light, hands, rainbows and unicorns. Instead, it is much more like entering a maze when you begin the process of recovery; you are not climbing a mountain where you will feel, with each step, a deep and abiding sense of progress and the inevitability of reaching your ultimate goal.

I couldn't help but be reminded of the maze in Harry Potter and the Goblet of Fire. As Dumbledore says in the film version: 'In the maze you'll find no dragons or creatures of the deep. Instead you'll face something even more challenging. You see, people **change** *in the maze.'*

'How can you succeed? It is not measured in those terms.' I think this is one of the most important lessons recovery has taught me, and perhaps one of the hardest to accept. People do change in this maze – but there's no enchanted Goblet to whisk us away – only, perhaps, the gradual realisation that we're no longer lost. —Patient N

The thing you face as you contemplate your future existence in remission is not whether the damage is reversible or not (it largely is in any case), but whether you can accommodate the fact that healing is often a process filled with chaos, crises and violence.

The processes that have maintained your life thus far must be destroyed to allow for new, and more resilient, processes to take their place to support remission. What has kept you together thus far as you sink slowly into the oblivion of an eating disorder will not take you forward to remission.

The recovery process is not without risk. Healing is a risky proposition. We have long ago lost contact with an ability to differentiate between symptoms that denote devolution of life systems and symptoms that denote rebuilding of life systems.

We have all convinced ourselves, especially in medicine, that stability is an ideal state. But stability and healing are often mutually exclusive states.

However in the final analysis, the pain you will experience in recovery commonly reflects healing but it might reflect the necessity of medical intervention for some. Trying to figure out when you need the experts to investigate your pain and when you need to leave it all to a natural healing process is problematic. It isn't always a "nothing to lose" situation to investigate pain that turns out to be utterly benign. It is beyond the scope of a guide like this one to offer any guidelines except to suggest you trust your instincts.

Types of pain that are common in recovery include:

- dull, aching pains associated with water retention, bone re-mineralization, and/or connective tissue repair (often sacroiliac and knee joints).

- tingling, numbness, sometimes sharp zapping pain, or prickling sensations associated with nervous system repair, most commonly experienced in the arms and hands, and lower legs and feet.

- bloating, cramping, either dull aches or sharp pains throughout the gut (although they should be temporary and never be increasing in intensity or duration).

There are also symptoms associated with cardiac damage due to restriction:

- tachycardia (the sensation of the heart speeding up or skipping a beat while you are at rest).

- bradycardia (an extremely low resting heart rate, classified as under 60 bpm) often misdiagnosed as a sign of athletic health however specific QT-interval prolongation[87] will confirm it's not athletic fitness at work. Often this is accompanied by low blood pressure.

- orthostatic hypotension and/or postural orthostatic tachycardia syndrome: either feeling dizzy or faint going from lying to sitting or sitting to standing, or a racing heart when going from lying to sitting or sitting to standing.

Rest and re-feeding tends to resolve all of the above symptoms for patients in recovery from an eating disorder. However, only your medical doctor can assess whether any pain or symptom you experience during recovery can be allowed to resolve in due time or should be addressed with appropriate intervention to maintain both your safety and ongoing quality of life.

Sexy bricks

February 23, 2012 - Kayebunny

Here is a note about sex drive: When it comes back, it comes back all at once. It will hit you like a truck full of bricks. Sexy, sexy bricks.

Kayebunny captured the welcome shock that is the return of libido, for both men and women in recovery, on the Eating Disorder Institute forums so well that "sexy bricks" became the go-to heading for any community members looking to discuss sex and recovery on the forums.

Most do indeed experience a return of their sex drive with an intensity best described as "being hit by a truck." For those at ease with their sexuality and sexual identity, the suddenness and intensity of the return of sexual interest and desire might still be disorienting, given possibly years of unending disinterest, going through the motions, and perhaps even starvation-induced pain and discomfort during sex too.

And it can also be a decidedly frightening and unwelcome experience for some. For those where sexual abuse or trauma features in their past, restrictive eating behaviors might have ended up inextricably linked with coping with the legacy of such abuse or trauma.

Again, trauma and abuse do not cause an eating disorder, but for some predisposed individuals they may activate and/or reinforce the condition.

There is obviously some urgency for involving a qualified therapist or counselor if trauma and abuse have resulted in a very damaged sense of your own sexuality and sexual identity. However, there is also tremendous value in involving a therapist or counselor even when the return of libido is a welcome addition to your life. As mentioned in chapter 2, an eating disorder usually hijacks maturation and development and therefore your returning sense of sexuality might feel awkward, immature and unwieldy in ways that working through the challenges with a therapist can greatly improve.

Neither/nor second phase in recovery

Assuming a patient has managed to wade through all the physical discomfort of the first phase in the Homeodynamic Recovery Method, she will tend to turn her attention to the physical shape and lingering symptoms in this neither/nor second phase in the recovery process.

I can often identify someone on sight who is living within the neither/nor space. It is difficult to describe, but patients genuinely appear unformed—not misshapen, just lacking definition and subtle age-appropriate refinement in shape. The term we have settled on is: adult-sized toddler.

The body preferentially lays down fat around the midsection to insulate vital organs from hypothermia.[88] And unfortunately, many relapse at this point because the level of distress is high and associated with a sense that the shape they have is permanent. The face, neck, shoulders, and abdomen appear out of proportion. This is a normal and transient phase in recovery, but it is difficult to maintain enough mental and emotional distance to appreciate that the body is healing. The even redistribution of the fat around the midsection to the rest of the body occurs if you persist right to the final phase.[89]

The second phase is marked with lingering and irksome symptoms *(see the previous section "Conundrum of pain" for details)* combined with the disproportionate fat mass around the trunk of the body. The honeymoon phase of actually thrilling to that food intake is a distant memory. Patients in the second phase tend to remain very focused on the physical experience of recovery.

Some patients will complain of boredom with food in phases two and three. Others will complain of no longer being hungry for the food. Many will ask if this is a sign that they "are done" with recovery. Expressions of boredom and disconnection with hunger originate with anxiety and are not signs of "being done."

Identifying boredom is negatively correlated with mood labeling and with flow. [§§,90] These negative correlations are important because the state of boredom is often viewed as a trigger for anxiety, but it is quite likely that boredom is a mislabeled mood that actually should be identified as underlying anxiety. It is very difficult to experience any hedonic (pleasant) connection when dealing with the physiological discomfort and arousal of a threat identification response. That means that losing interest in food could be the result

---

§§ Flow, in a psychological sense, refers to a sense of being completely immersed in the task at hand. The term "flow" comes from psychology professor Mihály Csíkszentmihályi. Do not ask me to pronounce that name.

of still maintaining a diet that is too bland and restricted in terms of food choice (keeping enjoyable foods off the list because of perceived threat) or that the anxiety associated with approaching and eating food has been misidentified as boredom.

Boredom in relation to the second phase of recovery is usually frank anxiety that makes it difficult to maintain connection with the hedonic value of food intake. And food is meant to be pleasant. Quoting myself here:

To assume that hedonic consumption of food is unnecessary to maintaining homeostasis, or homeodynamic balance, is to suggest that the evolutionarily older parts of our brain are unnecessary to our overall health and survival. To believe that conscious suppression of eating desires or intuitions is all that stands between us and chaotic weight fluctuations flies in the face of central nervous system biological fact.[91]

Must-be-done-by-now third phase of recovery

It is between phases two and three that a patient should seek appropriate counseling or therapeutic support to persist with the recovery effort to get to full remission, if she is not already receiving psychoeducational support. In fact, in order to shift into phase three, a patient has to move beyond the physical experience of recovery to address how her thoughts and emotions continue to reinforce behaviors that may keep her disconnected from her hunger. Feelings of frustration at having the process of recovery appear to stall or having unmet expectations of a "just-so" recovery process, can impede a patient's connection to hunger as readily as the states of anxiety and boredom.

Remember that the intake guidelines match what non–eating disordered individuals eat every day on average, so if you are unable to match that amount, the first line of investigation is to uncover how much lingering avoidance of food is at fault.

Although many patients have a far greater struggle to rest fully, even when they are able to feed and respond fully to hunger, it is the integral necessity for psychoeducational training and support that has so many stuck in a neither/nor phase. These individuals often contact me with ever increasing levels of despair and accusation that their recovery is not progressing as it does for everyone else.

There are many reasons why individuals in this situation will not seek out psychoeducational support, not the least of which is often the financial incapacity to pay for those services. However, on many occasions, the financial impact of seeing a therapist is not the defining factor in choosing not to build the third leg of getting to remission. There are options for getting therapy when money is tight, not the least of which is to look out various excellent workbooks that can be found on library shelves everywhere.

If you are feeling stuck then look to the likelihood that it is your assumptions, world view, and the cascade of practiced behaviors you have in response to those thoughts and feelings, that are getting in your way of moving forward into remission.

High-risk final phase to remission

If a patient manages to expend energy and focus on the brain retraining aspects of remission during the third phase, then the last phase to remission is in some ways the most rewarding and also the most dangerous.

When a patient has been advised to pursue a specific target weight as a marker of remission, or when she has treatment team members that have not recognized their own culturally steeped prejudice when it comes to obesity, then she will often be encouraged to stop eating so much and return to so-called maintenance intake and activity levels.

It is a recipe for fast, and often very severe, relapse. The minimum intake guidelines are designed for non-eating disorder healthy controls. Any intake amount below those averages is subclinical restriction. There is no scientific validity to the cultural construct that anyone must consciously restrict food intake to maintain her health and weight. Specifically, any recommendation for someone with a history of an eating disorder to restrict intake to maintain weight is simply dangerously unsound advice.

Even in the presence of a confirmed diagnosis of a competing chronic condition, few such conditions have morbidity or mortality issues that rest anywhere near the severity of an active eating disorder. Your medical advisors should therefore apply extreme caution even when modest improvements in mortality outcomes may be realized for some other chronic condition with the application of, most commonly, exercise.

A flare or relapse of an eating disorder is almost always not worth the risk in comparison to very subtle improvements in other chronic conditions that could also be realized without applying exercise or restricting dietary choice.

At this point in recovery, when potentially faced with these misguided suggestions to restrict, many patients will have temporarily overshot their optimal weight set point. While they have done all the hard work in therapy and counseling to reframe their innate self-worth as having nothing to do with numbers on the scale, they may find that suddenly loved ones and treatment teams alike are all in a tizzy over the weight.

Just as these patients start to feel at home in their own skins and are finally experiencing more energy, less pain and swelling, and feel well connected to hunger that takes them easily to the minimum intake guidelines (as expected), they are slammed by society's endemic levels of anxiety over all things to do with body weight. Everyone wants them to recover, but not too much. As with Patient E's observations at the beginning of chapter 2, it is very painful when those close to you cannot let go of their own prejudice to relish your improved state of mind and health.

It's not a comfortable space to be outside a cultural norm of any kind. There is a reason that the white rabbit lives within the Homeodynamic Recovery Method logo. As mentioned in the introduction of this handbook, the white rabbit references many literary metaphors, including its presence in the movie *The Matrix*. The protagonist in the movie, Neo, is told to follow the white rabbit (referencing Lewis Carroll's book *Alice's Adventures in Wonderland*) and, in making the decision to do so, he is quickly faced with the choice to remain safe and secure in his existing world, or to enter the complete unknown.

After this, there is no turning back.

You take the blue pill—the story ends, you wake up in your bed and believe whatever you want to believe.

You take the red pill—you stay in Wonderland and I show you how deep the rabbit-hole goes.

Remember: all I am offering is the truth. Nothing more.

Morpheus, The Matrix

Hunger

An eating disorder is not merely a condition that reflects brain chemistry; it resides in the mind, too. And therefore it can spread throughout the identity of self like a virus.

"I am the thin gal/guy and that's who I am."

"I am the fit gal/guy and that's who I am."

"I was always athletic. Even before the eating disorder."

"I never really ate much as a kid and was always naturally small."

"I like being lean."

Or, my favorite, paraphrased from an Eating Disorder Institute community member *learningtoaccept*:

"Everyone else big looks good but I don't because I'm a special snowflake."

That specialness allows you to hold yourself to a different standard, one you would never dream of applying to others. Usually this thought process allows someone to assure others that they are not fattist and don't hate fat people, but that they could not accept being fat for themselves.

All variations on these statements boil down to one thing: *my identity has been subsumed by the chronic condition I have*. Of course, that annexation of identity by an eating disorder is not exclusively driving the reinforcement of restrictive eating behaviors, but it plays its part in creating ambivalence in the patient for pursuing remission.

Hunger as acceptance

Imagine for a moment all the things we believe to be true about being fat in our society were applied to the way we view being thin. You are thin because you are irresponsible and don't take care to eat enough to stay healthy. It makes you a bad parent, partner, child, and friend. You are lazy and selfish. Friends pity you and feel sorry for your partner and your family: "How could you let yourself get so thin? I mean it's not rocket science, you just eat more and stop walking about so much for goodness' sake!" They tell you to get yourself together and that they are pointing out your sickly, stick-like appearance to you bluntly "for your own good."

Well, wouldn't that be disturbing! But, in such a society, the pressure you would feel to rectify your restrictive behaviors would be much more powerful than in the society in which you currently reside where you can easily hide the underlying misery of your condition with the veneer of looking like a beacon of self-discipline, moral authority, health, and well-being.

That is not to say that those with an eating disorder are not subjected to significant misunderstanding and abuse within society as well. There are plenty who would be able to list dozens of examples of being told that they just simply need to eat more and to stop being "so selfish." But generally speaking, the compliments received in the early phases of activation for achieving weight loss and "being healthy" provide powerful social acceptability reinforcements that would be impossible to brush aside for any human being (underlying eating disorder or not).

Then there is an additional truly deadly facet of our societal fear of fat: if you make a run for recovery from an eating disorder, then in fairly short order you may likely have parents, family members, friends, doctors, entire treatment teams, therapists, nurses, and even strangers on the street, suggest that you are likely done with your recovery and are maybe starting to get a bit (voice drops to whisper here) fat. I'll speak a bit more about this issue in chapter 6.

Hunger as distraction

And what of your personal life experiences of loneliness, pain, abuse, trauma, disappointments, failures, insecurities, feeling like an oddball, not fitting in, feeling desperate for approval, and all the other general challenges of navigating modern life? These don't matter much when the mind is filled with the complexities of avoiding food and yet needing to eat. It is yet another reason why the third leg of psychoeducational training and support is a non-negotiable facet of reaching full remission.

Keeping in mind that energy deficiency itself creates emotional blunting for those with eating disorders, the initial onset of the disorder creates a lot of psychological relief. You cannot feel when you are energy deficient.

A culture fixated on female thinness is not an obsession about female beauty, but an obsession about female obedience. Dieting is the most potent political sedative in women's history; a quietly mad population is a tractable one. — Naomi Woolf

I think that quote applies to everyone. Given that our society is developing increasing levels of wealth disparity, I think obedience and sedation take on validity for all. Hunger flattens righteous anger and removes any discomfort of needing to resolve unacceptable situations within your own life: toxic relationships, toxic jobs, buried trauma, and/or an undefined self.

Hunger is unique

The way your mind is interwoven with the neurobiology of your condition is truly unique. Some of the above broad facets of the ways in which the mind reinforces the condition may ring true for you, or they may have nothing to do with the expression of your particular eating disorder whatsoever.

However it is important to identify the ways in which your mind reinforces restriction. If you attend to the physical aspects of recovery, rest, and re-feeding, while neglecting to identify and retrain the mind's connection to reinforcement of restriction, then relapse is usually right around the corner.

I harp on this topic constantly, but it cannot be restated enough:

Pursue counseling.

No money for counseling? Do an online search for services that are provided at greatly reduced cost or no charge. Borrow from family. See if your school, college, or workplace offers, or covers the cost of, any counseling services. Go to the library and get all the workbooks and books available on self-help anxiety treatments. Too starved to read or think? Get book tapes on those topics instead.

Anxiety lessens with confrontation and worsens with avoidance.

If you are afraid of butter, use cream. — *Julia Child*

Humans, as social primates, are capable of caring for their vulnerable kin because resilience ebbs and flows in us all at different points in our lives. And vulnerability is not about being sick or ill; it is about being afraid to explore.

Obviously signing up for the first trip to Mars is not the only way to embrace exploration as a way to develop increased resilience. Our tolerance for exploration is variable from one individual to the next.

The fear of exploration has many sources, but chief among those reasons is failing to hold a sense of self lightly in one's mind. And often anxiety generates a sense of self that is disproportionately based on the "cannot," "do not," "will not" labels and classifications of who we are.

If we presume that someone with an eating disorder has a powerful threat identification system that actually inhibits the reward identification system, then getting to remission means nudging oneself to a space where rewards are even feasible before they will be dependably sought out. And yet again, psychoeducational training will offer that safe space for exploration and development in these areas.

End Notes for Chapter Four

1. Jerry F. Franklin, J. A. MacMahon, F. J. Swanson, J. R. Sedel, "Ecosystem responses to the eruption of Mount St. Helens," *National Geographic Research* 1 (1985): 198-216.

2. Cecilia Bergh, Ulf Brodin, Greger Lindberg, and Per Södersten, "Randomized controlled trial of a treatment for anorexia and bulimia nervosa," *Proceedings of the National Academy of Sciences* 99, no. 14 (2002): 9486-9491.

3. Ann Von Holle, Andréa Poyastro Pinheiro, Laura M. Thornton, Kelly L. Klump, Wade H. Berrettini, Harry Brandt, Steven Crawford, Scott Crow, Manfred M. Fichter, Katherine A. Halmi, Craig Johnson, Allan S. Kaplan, Pamela Keel, Maria LaVia, James Mitchell, Michael Strober, D. Blake Woodside, Walter H. Kaye, and Cynthia M. Bulik, "Temporal patterns of recovery across eating disorder subtypes," *Australian and New Zealand Journal of Psychiatry* 42, no. 2 (2008): 108-117.

4. Jennifer Couturier and James Lock, "What is recovery in adolescent anorexia nervosa?" *International Journal of Eating Disorders* 39, no. 7 (2006): 550-555.

5. Michael Strober, Roberta Freeman, and Wendy Morrell, "The long-term course of severe anorexia nervosa in adolescents: Survival analysis of recovery, relapse, and outcome predictors over 10–15 years in a prospective study," *International Journal of Eating Disorders* 22, no. 4 (1997): 339-360.

6. Tabita Björk and Gerd Ahlström, "The Patient's Perception of Having Recovered From an Eating Disorder," *Health Care for Women International* 29, 8-9 (2008): 926-944.

7. Andrea K. Garber, Nobuaki Michihata, Katherine Hetnal, Mary-Ann Shafer, and Anna-Barbara Moscicki, "A Prospective Examination of Weight Gain in Hospitalized Adolescents With Anorexia Nervosa on a Recommended Refeeding Protocol," *Journal of Adolescent Health* 50, no. 1 (2012): 24-29.

8. Melissa Whitelaw, Heather Gilbertson, Pei-Yoong Lam, and Susan M. Sawyer, "Does aggressive refeeding in hospitalized adolescents with anorexia nervosa result in increased hypophosphatemia?" *Journal of Adolescent Health* 46, no. 6 (2010): 577-582.

9. Joanna E. Steinglass, Robyn Sysko, Deborah Glasofer, Anne Marie Albano, H. Blair Simpson, and B. Timothy Walsh, "Rationale for the application of exposure and response prevention to the treatment of anorexia nervosa," *International Journal of Eating Disorders* 44, no. 2 (2011): 134-141.

10. Tom Hildebrandt, Terri Bacow, Mariana Markella, and Katharine L. Loeb, "Anxiety in anorexia nervosa and its management using family-based treatment," *European Eating Disorders Review* 20, no. 1 (2012): e1-e16.

11. Frances A. Carter, Virginia V. W. McIntosh, Peter R. Joyce, Patrick F. Sullivan, and Cynthia M. Bulik, "Role of exposure with response prevention in cognitive–behavioral therapy for bulimia nervosa: Three-year follow-up results," *International Journal of Eating Disorders* 33, no. 2 (2003): 127-135.

12. Joanna Steinglass and Sarah Parker, "Using Exposure and Response Prevention Therapy to Address Fear in Anorexia Nervosa," *Eating Disorders Review* 22, no. 5 (2011): 1-5.

13. Laeeq U.R. Khan, Jamil Ahmed, Shakeeb Khan, and John MacFie, "Refeeding Syndrome: A Literature Review," *Gastroenterology Research and Practice* 2011 (2011): 1-6.

14. Akwasi Afriyie Boateng, Krishnan Sriram, Michael M. Meguid, and Martin Crook, "Refeeding syndrome: Treatment considerations based on collective analysis of literature case reports," *Nutrition* 26, no. 2 (2010): 156-167.

15. Rollyn M. Ornstein, Neville H. Golden, Marc S. Jacobson, and I. Ronald Shenker, "Hypophosphatemia during nutritional rehabilitation in anorexia nervosa: implications for refeeding and monitoring," *Journal of Adolescent Health* 32, no. 1 (2003): 83-88.

16. Akwasi Afriyie Boateng, Krishnan Sriram, Michael M. Meguid, and Martin Crook, "Refeeding syndrome: Treatment considerations based on collective analysis of literature case reports," *Nutrition* 26, no. 2 (2010): 156-167.

17. Philip S. Mehler, Cynthia Crews, and Kenneth Weiner, "Bulimia: Medical Complications," *Journal of Women's Health* 13, no. 6 (2004): 668-675.

18. Hisham M. Mehanna, Jamil Moledina, and Jane Travis, "Refeeding syndrome: what it is, and how to prevent and treat it," *British Medical Journal* 336, no. 7659 (2008): 1495-1498.

19. Amy Colwell, "Refeeding Syndrome Symptoms," *EatingDisorders Online* , last modified September 12, 2011, http://www.eatingdisorder-sonline.com/articles/anorexia/refeeding-syndrome-symptoms.

20. C. Laird Birmingham and S. Gritzner, "How does zinc supplementation benefit anorexia nervosa?" *Eating and Weight Disorders-Studies on Anorexia, Bulimia and Obesity* 11, no. 4 (2006): e109-e111.

21. Barbara E. Golden and M. H. N. Golden, "Effect of zinc on lean tissue synthesis during recovery from malnutrition," *European Journal of Clinical Nutrition* 46, no. 10 (1992): 697-706.

22. C. L. Birmingham, D. Puddicombe, and J. Hlynsky, "Hypomagnesemia during refeeding in anorexia nervosa," *Eating and Weight Disorders-Studies on Anorexia, Bulimia and Obesity* 9, no. 3 (2004): 236-237.

23. Akwasi Afriyie Boateng, Krishnan Sriram, Michael M. Meguid, and Martin Crook, "Refeeding syndrome: Treatment considerations based on collective analysis of literature case reports," *Nutrition* 26, no. 2 (2010): 156-167.

24. Stacey McCray, Sherrie Walker, and Carol Rees Parrish, "Much ado about refeeding," *Practical Gastroenterology* 29, no. 1 (2005): 26-44.

25. A. P. Winston, C. P. Jamieson, W. Madira, N. M. Gatward, and R. L. Palmer, "Prevalence of thiamin deficiency in anorexia nervosa," *International Journal of Eating Disorders* 28, no. 4 (2000): 451-454.

26. Katherine A. Beals and Melinda M. Manore, "Nutritional Status of Female Athletes with Subclinical Eating Disorders," *Journal of the Academy of Nutrition and Dietetics* 98, no. 4 (1998): 419-425.

27. Kristin L. Cobb, Laura K. Bachrach, Gail Greendale, Robert Marcus, Robert M. Neer, Jeri Nieves, Mary Fran Sowers, Bryron W. Brown Jr., Geetha Gopalakrishnan, Crystal Luetters, Heather K. Tanner , Bridget Ward, Jennifer L. Kelsey, "Disordered eating, menstrual irregularity, and bone mineral density in female runners," *Medicine & Science in Sports & Exercise* 35, no. 5 (2003): 711-719.

28. K-F. Kreitner, F. J. Schweden, T. Riepert, B. Nafe, and M. Thelen, "Bone age determination based on the study of the medial extremity of the clavicle," *European Radiology* 8, no. 7 (1998): 1116-1122.

29. Kathryn J. Zerbe, "Late Life Eating Disorders," *Eating Disorders Review* 24, no. 6 (2013): 3-5.

30. Dimitry A. Chistiakov, "Immunogenetics of Hashimoto's thyroiditis," *Journal of Autoimmune Diseases* 2 (2005): 1.

31. Peter N. Taylor, Ahmed Iqbal, Caroline Minassian, Adrian Sayers, Mohd S. Draman, Rosemary Greenwood, William Hamilton, Onyebuchi Okosieme, Vijay Panicker, Sara L. Thomas, and Colin Dayan, "Falling Threshold for Treatment of Borderline Elevated Thyrotropin Levels—Balancing Benefits and Risks: Evidence From a Large Community-Based Study," *JAMA Internal Medicine* 174, no. 1 (2014): 32-39.

32. Tomoko Wakasa, Masayuki Shintaku, Shinzo Tanaka, Koichiro Yamada, Yaqiong Li, and Kennichi Kakudo, "Morphological Changes of Follicular Cells in Hashimoto's disease: A Possible Cause of Overdiagnosis in Cytology," *Journal of Basic and Clinical Medicine* 2, no. 1 (2013): 12-16.

33. Nobuyuki Amino, Kiyoshi Miyai, Toshio Onishi, Takuma Hashimoto, Kayoko Arai, Kaichiro Ishibashi, and Yuichi Kumahara, "Transient hypothyroidism after delivery in autoimmune thyroiditis," *The Journal of Clinical Endocrinology & Metabolism* 42, no. 2 (1976): 296-301.

34. Khan Mohammad Sajid, Mehfooz Akhtar, and Ghulam Qadir Malik, "Ramadan fasting and thyroid hormone profile," *Journal of Pakistan Medical Association* 41, no. 9 (1991): 213-216.

35. Jara Nedvidkova, Hana Papezová, Martin Haluzik, and Vratislav Schreiber, "Interaction Between Serum Leptin Levels and Hypothalamo-Hypophyseal-Thyroid Axis in Patients with Anorexia Nervosa," *Endocrine Research* 26, no. 2 (2000): 219-230.

36. R. N. Clayton, V. Ogden, J. Hodgkinson, L. Worswick, D. A. Rodin, S. Dyer, and T. W. Meade, "How common are polycystic ovaries in normal women and what is their significance for the fertility of the population?" *Clinical Endocrinology* 37, no. 2 (1992): 127-134.

37. Ricardo Azziz, "Diagnosis of polycystic ovarian syndrome: the Rotterdam criteria are premature," *The Journal of Clinical Endocrinology & Metabolism* 91, no. 3 (2006): 781-785.

38. Julian H. Barth, Ephia Yasmin, and Adam H. Balen, "The diagnosis of polycystic ovary syndrome: the criteria are insufficiently robust for clinical research," *Clinical Endocrinology* 67, no. 6 (2007): 811-815.

39. Daniel J. Carlat, Carlos A. Camargo, and David B. Herzog, "Eating disorders in males: A report on 135 patients," *American Journal of Psychiatry* 154, no. 8 (1997): 1127-1132.

40. Gwyneth Olwyn, "Weight Gain Despite Calorie Restriction" *Eating Disorder Institute* (paper), June 13, 2015, https://www.edinstitute.org/paper/2015/6/13/gaining-weight-despite-calorie-restriction.

41. Harry E. Gwirtsman, Walter H. Kaye, Eva Obarzanek, David T. George, David C. Jimerson, and Michael H. Ebert, "Decreased caloric intake in normal-weight patients with bulimia: comparison with female volunteers," *The American Journal of Clinical Nutrition* 49, no. 1 (1989): 86-92.

42. Jane Wardle, "Compulsive eating and dietary restraint," *British Journal of Clinical Psychology* 26, no. 1 (1987): 47-55.

43. M. M. Hagan, P. K. Wauford, P. C. Chandler, L. A. Jarrett, R. J. Rybak, and K. Blackburn, "A new animal model of binge eating: key synergistic role of past caloric restriction and stress," *Physiology & Behavior* 77, no. 1 (2002): 45-54.

44. Tanja C. Adam and Elissa S. Epel, "Stress, eating and the reward system," *Physiology & Behavior* 91, no. 4 (2007): 449-458.

45. Leanne M. Redman, Leonie K. Heilbronn, Corby K. Martin, Lilian De Jonge, Donald A. Williamson, James P. Delany, Eric Ravussin, "Metabolic and Behavioral Compensations in Response to Caloric Restriction: Implications for the Maintenance of Weight Loss," *PLOS ONE* 4, no. 2 (2009): e4377.

46. Dale A. Schoeller, "Recent Advances from Application of Doubly Labeled Water to Measurement of Human Energy Expenditure," *The Journal of Nutrition* 129, no. 10 (1999): 1765-1768.

47. Maciej S. Buchowski, "Doubly labeled water is a validated and verified reference standard in nutrition research." *The Journal of Nutrition* 144, no. 5 (2014): 573-574.

48. Statistics Canada, "Canadian Community Health Survey Cycle 2.2, Nutrition Focus (Revised 2008)," *Health Canada*, last modified March 15, 2012, https://www.canada.ca/en/health-canada/services/food-nutrition/food-nutrition-surveillance/health-nutrition-surveys/canadian-community-health-survey-cchs/canadian-community-health-survey-cycle-2-2-nutrition-focus-food-nutrition-surveillance-health-canada.html.

49. Public Health England, *Food Standards Agency* , "National diet and nutrition survey: results from years 1-4 (combined) of the rolling programme (2008/2009 – 2011/12)," (executive summary, United Kingdom, 2014), 11.

50. Jacqueline D. Wright, Chia-Yih Wang, Jocelyn Kennedy-Stephenson, R. Bethene Ervin, "Dietary Intake of Ten Key Nutrients for Public Health, United States: 1999–2000," *Advance Data from Vital and Health Statistics, Centers for Disease Control and Prevention*, no. 334 (2003): 1-4.

51. Dale A. Schoeller, "How accurate is self-reported dietary energy intake?" *Nutrition Reviews* 48, no. 10 (1990): 373-379.

52. James R. Hébert, Cara B. Ebbeling, Charles E. Matthews, Thomas G. Hurley, Yunsheng Ma, Susan Druker, Lynn Clemow, "Systematic errors in middle-aged women's estimates of energy intake: comparing three self-report measures to total energy expenditure from doubly labeled water," *Annals of Epidemiology* 12, no. 8 (2002): 577-586.

53. I. Asbeck, M. Mast, A. Bierwag, J. Westenhöfer, K. J. Acheson, and M. J. Müller, "Severe underreporting of energy intake in normal weight subjects: use of an appropriate standard and relation to restrained eating," *Public Health Nutrition* 5, no. 5 (2002): 683-690.

54. Reinhard J. Tuschl, Petra Platte, Reinhold G. Laessle, Willibald Stichler, and Karl-Martin Pirke, "Energy expenditure and everyday eating behavior in healthy young women," *The American Journal of Clinical Nutrition* 52, no. 1 (1990): 81-86.

55. Dale A. Schoeller, "Recent Advances from Application of Doubly Labeled Water to Measurement of Human Energy Expenditure," *The Journal of Nutrition* 129, no. 10 (1999): 1765-1768.

56. Anders M. Sjödin, Agneta B. Andersson, Jeanette M. Högberg, and Klaas R. Westerterp, "Energy balance in cross-country skiers: a study using doubly labeled water," *Medicine and Science in Sports and Exercise* 26, no. 6 (1994): 720-724.

57. M. Yao, M. A. McCrory, G. Ma, Y. Li, G. G. Dolnikowski, and S. B. Roberts, "Energy requirements of urban Chinese adults with manual or sedentary occupations, determined using the doubly labeled water method," *European Journal of Clinical Nutrition* 56, no. 7 (2002): 575-584.

58. Nancy F. Butte, William W. Wong, Margarita S. Treuth, Kenneth J. Ellis, and E. O'Brian Smith, "Energy requirements during pregnancy based on total energy expenditure and energy deposition," *The American Journal of Clinical Nutrition* 79, no. 6 (2004): 1078-1087.

59. Leslie O. Schulz and Dale A. Schoeller, "A compilation of total daily energy expenditures and body weights in healthy adults," *The American Journal of Clinical Nutrition* 60, no. 5 (1994): 676-681.

60. Linda G. Bandini, Dale A. Schoeller, Helen N. Cyr, and William H. Dietz, "Validity of reported energy intake in obese and nonobese adolescents," *The American Journal of Clinical Nutrition* 52, no. 3 (1990): 421-425.

61. Sandrine Lioret, Mathilde Touvier, Morgan Balin, Inge Huybrechts, Carine Dubuisson, Ariane Dufour, Mélanie Bertin, Bernard Maire, and Lionel Lafay, "Characteristics of energy under-reporting in children and adolescents," *British Journal of Nutrition* 105, no. 11 (2011): 1671-1680.

62. Helen Crawley and Rita Shergill-Bonnert, "The nutrient and food intakes of 16–17 year old female dieters in the UK," *Journal of Human Nutrition and Dietetics* 8, no. 1 (1995): 25-34.

63. H. Crawley and C. Summerbell, "The nutrient and food intakes of British male dieters aged 16–17 years," *Journal of Human Nutrition and Dietetics* 11, no. 1 (1998): 33-40.

64. "National Health and Nutrition Examination Survey [NHANES] 2005-2006 Body Measurements (BMX_D)," *Centers for Disease Control and Prevention*, last modified November 2007, https://wwwn.cdc.gov/nchs/nhanes/2005-2006/BMX_D.htm.

65. Ibid.

66. Philip S. Mehler and Arnold E. Andersen, *Eating Disorders: a Guide to Medical Care and Complications, second edition* (Baltimore: John Hopkins University Press, 2010).

67. Gwyneth Olwyn, "Gaining Weight Despite Calorie Restriction." *The Eating Disorder Institute"* Eating Disorder Institute (paper), June 13, 2015, https://www.edinstitute.org/paper/2015/6/13/gaining-weight-despite-calorie-restriction.

68. Aurelia Nattiv, Anne B. Loucks, Melinda M. Manore, Charlotte F. Sanborn, Jorunn Sundgot-Borgen, and Michelle P. Warren, American College of Sports Medicine, "American College of Sports Medicine position stand. The female athlete triad," *Medicine & Science in Sports & Exercise* 39, no. 10 (2007): 1867-1882.

69. D. Grahame Hardie, John W. Scott, David A. Pan, and Emma R. Hudson, "Management of cellular energy by the AMP-activated protein kinase system," *FEBS letters* 546, no. 1 (2003): 113-120.

70. Jeffrey S. Flier, "Regulating energy balance: the substrate strikes back," *Science* 312, no. 5775 (2006): 861-864.

71. Regina C. Casper, Barbara Kirschner, Harold H. Sandstead, Robert A. Jacob, and John M. Davis, "An evaluation of trace metals, vitamins, and taste function in anorexia nervosa," *The American Journal of Clinical Nutrition* 33, no. 8 (1980): 1801-1808.

72. Owais B. Chaudhri, B. C. T. Field, and S. R. Bloom, "Gastrointestinal satiety signals," *International Journal of Obesity* 32 (2008): S28-S31.

73. Paul B. Pencharz and Maria Azcue, "Use of bioelectrical impedance analysis measurements in the clinical management of malnutrition," *The American Journal of Clinical Nutrition* 64, no. 3 (1996): 485S-488S.

74. Marie Valerie Moreno, Djamal-Dine Djeddi, and Michel Y. Jaffrin, "Assessment of body composition in adolescent subjects with anorexia nervosa by bioimpedance," *Medical Engineering & Physics* 30, no. 6 (2008): 783-791.

75. F. Boag, J. Weerakoon, J. Ginsburg, C. W. Havard, and P. Dandona, "Diminished creatinine clearance in anorexia nervosa: reversal with weight gain," *Journal of Clinical Pathology* 38, no. 1 (1985): 60-63.

76. Frédéric Evrard, Mariana Pinto da Cunha, Michel Lambert, and Olivier Devuyst, "Impaired osmoregulation in anorexia nervosa: a case–control study," *Nephrology Dialysis Transplantation* 19, no. 12 (2004): 3034-3039.

77. Haiyan Lu, Danping Huang, Richard M. Ransohoff, and Lan Zhou, "Acute skeletal muscle injury: CCL2 expression by both monocytes and injured muscle is required for repair," *The FASEB Journal* 25, no. 10 (2011): 3344-3355.

78. Peter J. Murray and Thomas A. Wynn, "Protective and pathogenic functions of macrophage subsets," *Nature Reviews Immunology* 11, no. 11 (2011): 723-737.

79. Paul B. Pencharz and Maria Azcue, "Use of bioelectrical impedance analysis measurements in the clinical management of malnutrition," *The American Journal of Clinical Nutrition* 64, no. 3 (1996): 485S-488S.

80. Stefan Ehrlich, Uwe Querfeld, and Ernst Pfeiffer, "Refeeding oedema: An important complication in the treatment of anorexia nervosa," *European Child & Adolescent Psychiatry* 15, no. 4 (2006): 241-243.

81. Masahiko Hirakawa, Takao Okada, Mitsuo Iida, Hajime Tamai, Nobuyuki Kobayashi, Tetsuya Nakagawa, and Masatoshi Fujishima, "Small bowel transit time measured by hydrogen breath test in patients with anorexia nervosa," *Digestive Diseases and Sciences* 35, no. 6 (1990): 733-736.

82. Michael Camilleri and Maria I. Vazquez-Roque , "Gastric Dysmotility at the Organ Level in Gastroparesis," in *Gastroparesis*, eds. Henry P,. Parkman and Richard W. McCallum (New York: Humana Press, 2012), 37-46.

83. Elizabeth Tabone, Janice Russell, and Herman Herzog, interview by Lynne Malcom, *All In The Mind: The starving brain*, ABC Radio, March 25, 2006 (1:00 p.m.), http://www.abc.net.au/radionational/programs/allinthemind/the-starving-brain/3303444.

84. Victor W. Swayze II, Arnold E. Andersen, Nancy C. Andreasen, Stephan Arndt, Yutaka Sato, and Steve Ziebell, "Brain tissue volume segmentation in patients with anorexia nervosa before and after weight normalization," *International Journal of Eating Disorders* 33, no. 1 (2003): 33-44.

85. Angela Wagner, Phil Greer, Ursula F. Bailer, Guido K. Frank, Shannan E. Henry, Karen Putnam, Carolyn C. Meltzer, Scott K. Ziolko, Jessica Hoge, Claire McConaha, and Walter H. Kaye, "Normal Brain Tissue Volumes after Long-Term Recovery in Anorexia and Bulimia Nervosa," *Biological Psychiatry* 59, no. 3 (2006): 291-293.

86. Gabriele Hörmannsperger, Thomas Clavel, and Dirk Haller, "Gut matters: Microbe-host interactions in allergic diseases," *The Journal of Allergy and Clinical Immunology* 129, no. 6 (2012): 1452-1459.

87. I. Swenne, and P. T. Larsson, "Heart risk associated with weight loss in anorexia nervosa and eating disorders: risk factors for QTc interval prolongation and dispersion," *Acta Paediatrica* 88, no. 3 (1999): 304-309.

88. Laurel Mayer, B. Timothy Walsh, Richard N. Pierson, Steven B. Heymsfield, Dympna Gallagher, Jack Wang, Michael K. Parides, Rudolph L. Leibel, Michelle P. Warren, Erin Killory, and Deborah Glasofer, "Body fat redistribution after weight gain in women with anorexia nervosa," *The American Journal of Clinical Nutrition* 81, no. 6 (2005): 1286-1291.

89. Laurel E. S. Mayer, Diane A. Klein, Elizabeth Black, Evelyn Attia, Wei Shen, Xiangling Mao, Dikoma C. Shungu, Mark Punyanita, Dympna Gallagher, Jack Wang, Steven B. Heymsfield, Joy Hirsch, Henry N. Ginsberg, and B. Timothy Walsh, "Adipose tissue distribution after weight restoration and weight maintenance in women with anorexia nervosa," *The American Journal of Clinical Nutrition* 90, no. 5 (2009): 1132-1137.

90. Mary B. Harris, "Correlates and Characteristics of Boredom Proneness and Boredom1," *Journal of Applied Social Psychology* 30, no. 3 (2006): 576-598.

91. Gwyneth Olwyn, "Emotional Eating" *Eating Disorder Institute* (psychology, bottom of page), March 11, 2013, https://www.edinstitute. org/blog/2013/4/23/emotional-eating-mindful-vs-mindfulness.

Chapter Five

Treatment Support & Science

August 20, 2012 - Pat

I went to the doctor this morning and I told him about my thoughts about food and exercise but he thinks I'm ok because I don't look underweight and said that it's normal to be worried about food and weight. He thinks it's all in my head and told me to calm down.[*]

As I mentioned in chapter 4, often a recovery effort to remission is derailed right on the final bend to the finish line because both loved ones and treatment teams are fussing about weight gain and wanting you to return to society's current concept of normal behaviors for eating a healthy (translation: restrictive) diet and exercising regularly because they genuinely care about your health.

As a patient advocate, I teach people to become aware of the power differential built within the patient/provider relationship and how best to navigate the need for practitioner expertise while supporting the need for adequate boundaries that maintain your own best health care interests.

---

[*] The Eating Disorder Institute forum post.

Credentials and bell curves

Yet another bell-shaped curve looms as we consider credentials versus competence.

It is important to understand that credentials do not reveal competence. With all health care professionals, their credentials confirm that a form of legal recourse is available to you as a patient, should the care you receive be substandard or cause you harm in some way.

Credentials indicate that a person has gone through a formal education program of some sort. Inherent in that education program may or may not be a combination of classroom and practical training, but all programs will include some kind of formal assessment or testing against the body of knowledge that was imparted to the student. Assuming the student passes the assessment and testing then he or she has graduated.

From there, the vast majority of health care professionals will also require a period of active and supervised practice, perhaps as an intern or junior practitioner. Usually after a set period of hours is achieved, the practitioner is then eligible to apply for full credentialed status with a governing body of his or her peers. These colleges or professional associations have codes of conduct to which the members must adhere. In return, the associations provide opportunities for continuing education and peer support.

Nothing within that entire process will reveal to a patient the level of competence any individual health care practitioner may or may not have. And while many will argue that grade point averages will reveal superior skill sets, in fact they reveal an affinity for absorbing, retaining, and regurgitating a body of knowledge; and rather importantly, practice is a skill that is entirely distinct from absorbing, retaining, and regurgitating.

Competence resides on that ever-handy bell-shaped curve of human attributes. The vast majority of health care practitioners are of average competence and skill. A small minority will offer exceptional competence and skill, and so too will a small minority be worrisomely incompetent.

Accepting that credentials will merely provide you with legal recourse should your care be substandard will mean that you can move forward to making your own investigations to uncover competence and ability.

The power differential that is inherent in our relationships with professional service providers in general, and with health care service providers in particular, means that trying to assess competency is quite difficult. It often feels rude to ask a lot of questions and the practitioner might tell you outright she finds your questions rude, invasive, and unacceptable. However, a practitioner that will not answer questions you deem appropriate† should not get through your own gating process for determining who is best suited to work with you.

---

† Obviously a practitioner has every right to refuse to answer inappropriate questions. Questions about the personal lives of practitioners are inappropriate. However it can often be appropriate to ask whether they have any personal ethics or values that might conflict with your care needs. Areas where this might be of concern include reproductive health, family planning, and, (when applicable) the need for religious guidance that will align with your faith.

Kissing toads

You can't know it all. And even if you knew everything that anyone else knows (which you can't, so stop worrying about it), you still wouldn't know what you need to know to help many patients.

Perri Klass in A Not Entirely Benign Procedure[1]

Many looking for a primary care physician, dietician, and therapist to help with the process of recovery to remission tend to lean toward wanting to hire those specializing in eating disorders. Common sense would suggest that practitioners with specialization have a greater depth of subject area expertise to guide the patient through the recovery process.

Yet specialization necessitates exceptional competence and a great bedside manner, as it tends to make a practitioner far more vulnerable to believing she knows everything. When you involve a practitioner with absolutely no background in the field in question, but she has general curiosity and an interest in you as a person, then often the outcomes will be much more satisfactory to you.

As Perri Klass reminds specialists in the quote above: *you still wouldn't know what you need to know to help many patients.* Average specialists can readily fall into the trap of believing they already know what they need to know. They know everything. An exceptional specialist will always assume she has to learn more in order to help you.

The exceptional practitioners I know in the field of eating disorders are mind-blowingly good and about as easy to find as red diamonds. Sadly few patients will ever have access to working with these rare finds.

In the absence of working with an exceptional eating disorder specialist, your needs might be much better served working with an exceptional generalist—although these too are rare compared to their average counterparts, they are still easier to find than exceptional specialists.

These days you often fill out questionnaires before you so much as step into the health care practitioner's office. A well-designed questionnaire will help a practitioner understand more about your specific needs. However, what the practitioner needs to know about you and what you need to know about her are two distinct things.

An initial consultation with any health care practitioner should not involve any biomarker screening: no blood pressure measurements, no weighing, no height checking, no urine samples... nothing along those lines.‡ When you set an appointment with a new practitioner, make that requirement clear. You wish to consult with the practitioner so that you and she might determine if it's a good fit.

The established power differential becomes too great if you are first required to fill out their questionnaires, and then also submit to initial biomarker screening (usually undertaken by a medical aide) before even sitting down with the practitioner. The psychological impacts of providing extensive information before you receive the information you need is simply not conducive to respecting the ultimate decision-making control you have over your own body. Until you agree to work with the practitioner your body is off-limits.

---

‡ Obviously in emergent situations it is imperative the treatment team receive immediate feedback regarding your biomarkers, so this applies only to office consultations and not emergency department visits.

Your assessment of any potential health care provider begins from the moment you make your first contact with her office. When calling to book an initial consultation, jot down your initial impressions on a notepad:

1. Was the phone answered promptly?

2. Were you on hold with a recorded message that gave you some sense of how long you might be waiting to speak with someone?

3. When you spoke with the receptionist, did he put you at ease and express politeness and consideration?

You will often be asked to come to your appointment a few minutes early so that you might fill out their questionnaires. Be respectful of that request and do show up early. While you are filling out the questionnaire, bring your own notepad and mark down whether any question is actually seeking input about your concerns (providing enough room for you to answer in your own words); your reasons for seeking out the services of this particular practitioner; and whether you are asked to provide any input on your preferred style of interaction when it comes to the provision of care in question.

Frankly, I have yet to see any health care practitioner include that final, and very important, question on a questionnaire with the exception of one exceptional dentist I know. His new patient questionnaire also asks whether there are any anxieties or past experiences that you would like to make them aware of as well.

If you are escorted into an examination room and asked to step on a scale or roll up your sleeve, then inform the assistant that you are there for an initial consultation and your responses to the questionnaire will suffice until such time as you and the practitioner meet and mutually agree that working together seems like a good idea. I've actually done this myself and the nurse was understandably piqued but complied. That initial interface ended up merely being a reflection of the fact that the specialist himself had a notably "slab-o-meat" approach to his interactions with patients. Needless to say, I did not work with him beyond that consult.

Ideally the initial consultation should take place in a private office space and not an examination room. However, many practitioners use their office spaces such that private patient information is too readily visible to outside visitors (i.e., their desks are covered in patient files). If your initial consultation does take place within the examination room, be aware that the examination space heightens the power differential. In these cases, you will want the practitioner to be working a little harder to create an unimposing environment where you feel at ease. Some examples of neutralizing the power differential within an examination room include:

- chairs at the same height for both you and the doctor,

- you're not on the examination table or disrobed in any way,

- the practitioner introduces herself with first and last name, and not her honorific (i.e. not *Dr.* Soandso),

- she requests further clarification from you rather than targeting yes/no questions at you,

- she acknowledges your agenda for seeking her input and confirms her understanding of this by paraphrasing it back to you.[2,3]

Few of us have ever had the opportunity to learn how we might interview and assess a health care provider's potential for helping us meet our health care goals and therefore we have no guidelines or tools with which to accomplish a suitable interview. So we all tend to simply rush into discussing the immediate health issue at hand.

Unless you are lucky enough to engage with a practitioner who will facilitate your process of assessing their usefulness and compatibility with you, it's likely you will leave the office feeling you forgot to ask all the important questions. To help with this challenge, practitioner questionnaires for assessing a physician, therapist, and dietician are available to download from the Eating Disorder Institute website under the Resources section. Unfortunately you won't be handing those questionnaires over the practitioner for them to fill out; rather the questionnaire will help you shape the questions you ask during your consultation. Make notes as you go using the practitioner questionnaire as your guideline, and your decision to engage with them further or not, should be facilitated by reviewing those notes.

Consider a common analogy I use for determining whether or not to continue working with a professional: yellow card/red card. As is the case with fouls given in soccer, a yellow card is a warning while a red card means game over for that player.

An example of a yellow card infraction with a professional might be that a therapist begins an initial meeting by asking you to step on a scale. If you refuse and the introductory meeting and assessment appears to continue reasonably well, then it's likely worth returning for a subsequent visit to confirm whether that infraction was just an aberration or indicates a more broad approach that will not suit you.

Red cards are reserved for outright rudeness or contempt, and it's wise to end the consultation immediately when that happens.

In addition to the soccer analogy, I use one other analogy when it comes to paying attention to your instinct. I call it the ski-boot rule. If you rent your gear at the top of the mountain, and you're trying on rental ski boots, you have to pay close attention to the slightest twinge or pinching sensation you feel when the boot is on your foot. It's guaranteed that any slight discomfort at the top of the run will become excruciatingly, blood-blisteringly miserable halfway down that run. The ski-boot rule is a warning to never, never ignore your instinct.

We can all second-guess ourselves. There will be a million reasons why we think we should persist. You can usually put these reasons into one of two separate buckets. The first bucket means that you can still move forward because you have insufficient data and the second bucket means the issue is an absolute deal breaker.

Any doubt that leaves you feeling desperate, hopeless, or that you have run out of options and must therefore persist with the practitioner you don't like, most definitely goes into the second bucket. Such defeatist feelings will inevitably mean bad judgment and worse decisions will follow.

Conversely, if you can identify both good points and worrisome points from your initial interaction with a practitioner, then that interaction might be placed in the first bucket. It should be okay to continue working with the practitioner to get further information and clarification.

Deal breakers include a practitioner being dismissive of your questions or concerns, showing contempt, irritation or impatience, or just being plain rude.

It won't need to be said, but obviously you must treat a practitioner with the same respect you expect to receive from her. Be punctual. If you are running late, call ahead to the office with an explanation and apology. If her office has cancellation policies that mean insufficient notice will require you to pay for a missed appointment, then do so without complaint. If you are late, then anticipate your appointment might be shorter or you might be bumped in the schedule and therefore have a longer wait in the lobby. Respect the office policies and signage at all times. If you find yourself feeling resentful or retaliatory because you feel your practitioner is never on time or too distracted or uninvolved when you meet, then don't take that out on the front office staff. Instead, bring it up directly with the practitioner at the next appointment.

Just as you may decide to effectively fire your health care practitioner (by choosing not to return), practitioners have increasingly gotten in the habit of firing patients. While in some cases patients are told not to return to the practice because they have been violent or abusive to the practitioner and/or her staff, the most common reason for firing a patient is noncompliance. Noncompliance means that the patient is not following the health care practitioner's treatment recommendations.

A word on the increased prevalence of firing noncompliant patients: I find this trend sinister and unacceptable within health care. Here's the common definition of compliance: *inclined to agree with others or obey rules, especially to an excessive degree; acquiescent.*

An acquiescent patient will not likely realize optimal health outcomes; but she will ensure legally defensible health care oversight for the entities or organizations tasked with assigning a particular course of treatment or treatments to said patient.

This increasing trend for wanting compliant patients fails to encompass the far more serious cost and mortality implications of iatrogenic outcomes (injury or death directly as a result of medical treatment). There are an estimated 783,936 deaths directly attributable to medical intervention in the United States each year and there's evidence this estimate might be impacted by known underreporting of somewhere between 5% to 20%.[4]

I wholeheartedly agree with noted bioethicist Søren Holm who has this to say about patient noncompliance:

It is not patients who should comply with their doctors' demands, but doctors who should comply with their patients' informed and considered desires.[5]

Kissing toads, in the title of this section, refers to a much-loved quip that you have to kiss a lot of toads before you find that frog that turns into your prince(ss). Unfortunately, this quip is borne out when attempting to find the right treatment team for you. When you identify the toad, then just put it down and keep moving on. You'll find the right treatment support eventually.

Therapeutic options and treatment modalities

As I mentioned in the previous chapter, a starving brain does not work. Re-feeding and resting give the brain enough energy to allow a patient to engage in the retraining required to recalibrate the threat identification system to be less twitchy and more balanced with the reward identification system.

The brain is only 2% of your body by weight, but it requires 20% of the energy you take in.[6] The brain is monstrously impacted by restriction of food intake. All of the psychological treatment modalities and therapeutic mind retraining techniques are quite literally unthinkable during active restriction.

The ability to think bounces back quickly when re-feeding is fully underway. You will find yourself thinking more clearly as you re-feed; however there is often a punishing level of exhaustion in the initial 4–8 weeks of recovery. Therefore, looking for a counselor or therapist to work with beginning at the 2-month mark of recovery (approximately) means you will not be fighting through your exhaustion to make therapy appointments. Just to be clear, the exhaustion lasts much longer than 8 weeks, but for most patients after 8-weeks in recovery, it is feasible to negotiate regular counseling visits.

Different treatment modalities (programs or approaches) have different value depending on the patient's issues and preferences.

Cognitive behavioral therapy

The most convenient and common go-to for treatment is cognitive behavioral therapy (CBT). It's convenient because its prevalence is high (i.e., many practitioners are trained in this modality) and it's common because it has evidence-based outcomes for the treatment of anxiety disorders and eating disorders.[7,8,9,10] Even an online delivery format has been investigated thoroughly for CBT and has strong outcomes for anxiety.[11]

CBT is a two-step process that addresses cognitive fallacies that lead to maladaptive behaviors. Specifically, we tend to believe everything we think. More importantly, we often believe everything we feel. The distinct advantage of owning a human brain is that it has the capacity to think about its thinking and think about its feelings. This skill is called metacognition.

I can feel sad and I can also think to myself, "I am feeling sad." Metacognition allows us to stop automatically believing everything we think or feel. CBT helps a patient to develop stronger metacognitive skills. Then she can identify a cognitive fallacy as it happens. The cognitive space of CBT therapy necessarily includes a requirement to be aware of thoughts and feelings without applying any judgment or effort to suppress them.

Once a patient has practiced identifying and naming thoughts and feelings as they occur, she then moves onto assessing those thoughts and feelings further. The therapist or counselor guides the patient through this process of questioning the validity of thoughts and feelings that trigger maladaptive behaviors.

Assuming the patient determines that the thoughts and feelings that drive maladaptive behaviors are false, she can then move onto the second part of CBT, namely retraining behaviors that are driven from false thoughts and feelings.

Behavior retraining is tough. It's like all learning efforts—the initial attempts to apply a new behavior in place of the old avoidant ones will be awkward and uncomfortable. While CBT can be self-directed through various excellent workbooks and self-help books out there, having a counselor or therapist encourage you through the behavior retraining can help you avoid getting stuck with cognitive awareness but no tangible improvements in new behavior application.

Many patients with eating disorders are sure that recovery is a matter of brute-force willpower. However, the act of suppressing the drive to act on a false thoughts and feelings (in this case, avoiding food), exhausts cognitive capability very quickly. Inevitably it leads to a surge in maladaptive avoidant behaviors and the patient feels defeated and ashamed.

CBT is a treatment modality that ensures the patient doesn't end up trying to crush the drive to avoid food (which is not feasible), but rather she learns to develop replacement behaviors once the cognitive fallacies have been identified and accepted.

The threat response fires up because you are in the presence of food and this generates a false set of thoughts, feelings, and physiological changes in the body. Becoming competent at meta-cognitively identifying that cascade and then learning to apply new behaviors where you approach and eat the food is the aim of CBT as applied for eating disorder treatment.

CBT is usually of short duration (10 to 16 sessions) and is not a passive treatment—meaning that the patient must follow through on homework assignments and practice the suggested techniques in order to realize her desired outcomes.

Dialectical behavior therapy

Dr. Marsha Linehan developed dialectical behavior therapy (DBT) primarily to treat patients with borderline personality disorder. Borderline personality disorder is a condition that is poorly understood and its diagnosis is often used within the psychiatric and psychological communities as a derogatory category assigned to patients who are difficult to treat and help.

Since its development, the application of DBT has expanded beyond its use for patients with diagnosed borderline personality disorder. Inherently, the structure of this treatment modality serves any patient with emotional dysregulation extremely well.

Emotional regulation, similar to the means by which children learn to speak, is likely a module within our brains optimized to accept relevant input within a timed window of early childhood development. This regulation includes a variety of emotional states such as fear, anger, guilt, shame, dissociation, and numbing.

As with all disorders, there are likely genetic predispositions that may be activated by numerous complex environmental inputs that will result in the onset of emotional dysregulation. The tryptophan hydroxylase-2 (TPH2) gene generates a rate-limiting enzyme for serotonin synthesis that modulates responses within the emotional structures of the brain. Initial genotype studies suggest the significant presence of variants of that TPH2 gene for patients dealing with emotional dysregulation, when compared to healthy controls.[12]

One common environmental activator for emotional dysregulation in genetically prone individuals is the exposure to needy, neglectful, or abusive parents.[13] However, this may be attenuated or reinforced through peer interactions as the child develops.[14]

Emotional dysregulation may reflect a neural pattern called "kindling". Kindling is a concept applied to the experience of epilepsy and this concept may apply to many neural patterns beyond those experienced during epileptic seizure. Dr. Robert Post uses the frameworks of kindling and sensitization as models for better understanding all manner of emotional disorders.[15,16]

The essence of kindling, as it relates to epilepsy, is an after discharge whereby cell populations continue to fire in synchronous bursts after the stimulation has ceased. This synchronous firing is presumed to make it more likely that subsequent seizures will occur with progressively lower levels of stimulus. Emotional dysregulation appears well suited to the kindling model, as the experience is of an emotional state quickly being kindled into an inferno's worth of unpleasantness.

Another common environmental activator is experiencing or witnessing a traumatic event or events, leading to the development of a cluster of persistent emotions known as post-traumatic stress disorder (PTSD).

DBT integrates CBT with mindful awareness and distress tolerance techniques. The dialectic that is fundamental to this treatment modality is the balance of both acceptance and change strategies throughout the treatment process. It requires that the patient learn how to weigh and integrate conflicting or contradictory facts or ideas. Often a patient dealing with emotional dysregulation will experience sharp black-and-white thinking. If she fails to achieve a goal she has set for herself, then she becomes utterly despondent and believes herself incapable of any improvement at all. It takes practice to learn to accept falling short of a goal while also committing at the same time to keep striving to achieve that goal moving forward from that moment.

If you are dealing with suicidality, self-harming behaviors, or PTSD; you have a history of dealing with abuse in your childhood; and/or you just feel that your emotional responses seem outsized, then DBT (more than CBT) might offer you far better outcomes and an opportunity to reach remission from an eating disorder.

DBT has clinical trial data supporting its use for treatment of borderline personality disorder.[17,18] It also has some initial clinical data to support its value in treating PTSD related to childhood sexual abuse.[19] Initial case studies and open trials associated with the application of DBT for AN and BN, when other treatments (such as CBT) have failed, appear to offer reasonable outcomes in lowering symptoms associated with an eating disorder.[20,21]

DBT is necessarily of longer duration than CBT and involves more frequent individual sessions and additional group sessions. Recent studies are looking to shorten duration from 12 to 17 months to 6 months, given that initial randomized trial studies suggested most gains in DBT outcomes were realized within the first 4 months of treatment.[22]

Mindfulness or mindfulness-based stress reduction

Mindfulness or mindfulness-based stress reduction (MBSR) was originally developed from the Buddhist tradition of meditation. Dr. Jon Kabat-Zinn specifically defined the meditation technique as "mindfulness" because he wanted patients to avoid preconceived attitudes prominent at the time that meditation was too New Age to be of valid use. Kabat-Zinn founded the MBSR program in 1979 to help chronically ill patients, many with heart failure.

MBSR in treatment of eating disorders has small sample size clinical trials; however they do support its effectiveness for use in the application of reaching remission.[23]

Mindfulness encourages awareness and acceptance of thoughts, feelings and bodily sensations as they arise, and recognition of their impermanence. Mindfulness practitioners are taught to acknowledge and accept their experiences rather than to modify or suppress them. This change in one's relationship to present-moment experience has been described as "reperceiving" or "attentional control", and may facilitate more mindful behavioral choices. The set of skills associated with mindfulness can be taught independent of religious or cultural background, and in a variety of forms of interventions.[24]

MBSR can be framed as the application of metacognition to specifically reinforce the fluidity of thoughts, feelings, and states: "I feel really badly right now, but I know that this will pass." MBSR can be applied as a supportive technique for identifying and acknowledging the discomfort and agitation of facing food while agreeing not to act on that agitation by avoiding the food.

Exposure and response prevention

Exposure and response prevention (ERP) has already been mentioned in chapter 4. It is a specific type of CBT that is optimized to help those with obsessive-compulsive disorder (OCD) and those patients dealing with panic disorder and phobias.

As I said, it's a bit like desensitization or immunization therapies used to treat allergies. It's important to work with someone specifically trained in this treatment approach as it requires that the intensity be held below absolute maximal anxiety; the saturation remain constant; the duration be sufficient to achieve habituation; and that neutralization is blocked to avoid negating the process altogether.

In the 1960s, Drs. Raymond Levy and Victor Meyer developed an approach they called apotrepic therapy to help a patient prevent the application of rituals. The patients were monitored continually during waking hours, and even restrained (with their permission) to prohibit the application of rituals while they were exposed to situations that evoked the rituals in the first place. The rituals decreased, but instead of the expected increase in anxiety and depression, there was also a reduction in anxiety and depression.[25]

For OCD, therapy-guided exposure is superior to self-guided exposure.[26] As I mentioned in chapter 4, Dr. Steinglass and her colleagues have been at the forefront of assessing the validity of ERP for use in treating patients with both AN and BN.

Motivational interviewing

Motivational interviewing (MI) is a specific approach developed by Drs. William Miller and Stephen Rollnick originally framed to help those looking to overcome problem drinking. It is now an evidence-based treatment for those with substance abuse.

Dr. Janet Treasure, in her thorough article on MI, pointed out its value in application for any situation where there might be resistance to change; however she correctly points out that a patient rarely maintains a stable state of motivation, and therefore this manualized approach to helping a patient adopt new behaviors still requires an empathetic and sensitive therapist who can move back and forth along with the patient as she approaches and retreats from new behavior in nonlinear fashion.[27]

The essence of MI is to help a patient explore any ambivalence she may have toward replacing maladaptive coping mechanisms with adaptive and healthier behaviors.

A chronic condition of any kind is inherently interwoven into the patient's life and identity. As mentioned in chapter 4, many with an eating disorder will self-identify as "the thin one" or the "athletic one" or the "in-control, efficient and efficacious one." The process of achieving remission is not one of merely restoring weight and returning to normal and it's certainly not about bargaining with the eating disorder, either.

Patients will quite frequently ask me "Can I eat and not gain weight?" and I refer to these kinds of questions as bargaining with the eating disorder.

Questions such as these reveal the fact that the patient is dealing with ambivalence. While an eating disorder is not an addiction, it does have in common with addictions the fact that early in its activation and reinforcement, the patient experiences tangible benefits from the avoidance of food. She may feel more in control, less prone to uncomfortable or negative moods, and more energized and empowered. As the avoidance of food progresses, the negative impacts of that restriction start to accumulate. However, the patient persists in recalling the early days when restriction involved positive outcomes and she would like to return to that space without including all current negative impacts that are inexorably mounting up.

If you're feeling stuck, or have found that the anticipated tomorrow of starting to change behavior just never seems to arrive, then seeking a counselor with suitable MI training is likely going to be a good first step.

Eye movement desensitization and reprogramming

Eye movement desensitization and reprogramming (EMDR) is an established treatment for post-traumatic stress disorder (PTSD). It does have randomized controlled trials to support good outcomes for children with PTSD[28] and adults with PTSD.[29]

EMDR shows promise for patients with eating disorders as well. In one randomized trial where patients received standard residential treatment or standard residential treatment with EMDR, those with additional EMDR treatment reported less distress about negative body image and lower body dissatisfaction post 3-month and 12-month follow-up.[30] Generally, clinical trial data on EMDR suggests it has the greatest value for eating disorder patients in alleviating body image perception disturbances.

Emotional freedom technique

Emotional freedom technique (EFT) shares much in common with drug therapies for eating disorders. EFT is a dog's breakfast of acupuncture, neuro-linguistic programming, and energy therapy all melded into a process of applying self-administered therapy to alleviate distress. EFT is applied by tapping points on the body that presumably coincide with the body's "energy meridians" while repeating affirmations to alleviate distress. Often practitioners will incorporate the scientifically accredited EMDR process within EFT. Clinical trial data show EFT outcomes equivalent to placebo effect.[31]

Problematically for those with eating disorders, EFT can effectively replace safety behaviors and rituals with the tapping behaviors and that may circumvent the exposure necessary to actually approach and alleviate the threat identification response over time.

Talk therapies and finding what works for you

Talk therapy was once called psychoanalysis and is now referred to as psychodynamic therapy. This treatment approach has its roots in the work of both Sigmund Freud and Carl Jung.

While I have about as much use for Freud and Jung as I do for the DSM, I have been compelled to re-evaluate my overall dismissiveness of this treatment approach thanks to some rather ingenious and clever research originating from the University of British Columbia.

In a creatively designed trial, Dr. Ron Rensink and his colleagues were able to show that subjects increased accuracy from chance levels (50%) to well above chance (62.7%) when answering general knowledge questions as best as they could and then doing the same using a Ouija§ board.[32] And no, it was not an experiment looking to identify communication accuracy "from beyond the grave." Using a Ouija board actually accessed the subjects' own nonconscious thoughts.

While I am not sure that our nonconscious thoughts are modifiable in any way, there is no question that they exist. In fact the very presence of an eating disorder attests to the fact that non-conscious neural processes occur and misidentify food as a threat despite a clear conscious understanding that food is life sustaining and pleasurable.

Psychodynamic therapy offers a patient the opportunity to investigate all these facets of self. And if ultimately "knowing thyself" is a foundational pillar in either pursuing remission or knowing that remission is not a suitable state for you, then it's wise to recognize that psychodynamic therapy also has its place in the treatment of eating disorders as well.

While it is clear that evidence-based psychotherapy for eating disorders still rests firmly in the CBT camp, there are clearly numerous derivative and adjunct treatment modalities that hold evidence-based

§ Sometimes called a talking board, it was introduced in the 1890s in Pittsburgh as a harmless parlor game that provided a connection between the known and unknown and the material and immaterial [retrieved from: http://www.smithsonianmag.com/history/the-strange-and-mys-terious-history-of-the-ouija-board-5860627/?no-ist]

value. By seeking a counselor or therapist trained in several pertinent treatment modalities, you have the best chance of receiving personalized support that suits your specific treatment goals.

Additional treatment modalities

For further information on integrative cognitive affective therapy (ICAT), the Maudsley model for treatment of adults with anorexia (MANTRA), or FBT, please check out the series of posts on the Eating Disorder Institute on the University of California, San Diego Eating Disorders Conference 2014 (UCSD EDC2014). To clarify, MANTRA is designed for those with anorexia who are young adults but who are dealing with very severe and enduring anorexia that has either necessitated they remain living within the family home or dependent upon family for day-to-day living.

Drugs

There are actually no drugs available for treating an eating disorder. The prescriptions used to try to alleviate symptoms associated with an active eating disorder are either prescribed off-label, or are used to suppress or ease symptoms occurring from the physical damage due to restricting food intake. Off-label prescribing means that a drug that has regulatory approval for a specific condition is then prescribed for another unrelated condition in the absence of regulatory approval for its use in treating that unrelated condition.

Prescriptions for symptom management

There are several drug classes regularly prescribed to address gastrointestinal symptoms. These include the proton-pump inhibitor class used to reduce stomach acid; H2 receptor antagonists for acid reflux; the prokinetic agents used to deal with delayed gastric emptying; various laxative types that include softeners, lubricants, and osmotics; lavage agents if impaction risks are great; and cholinergic agonists for motility.

When autonomic nerve damage is present (gut motility is not functioning due to enteric nervous system damage), then tricyclic antidepressants may also be used to alleviate abdominal pain.

Drug classes prescribed to handle failing reproductive hormone levels, reproductive organ atrophy, and absent sex drive are recognizable to most. Oral contraceptives are often prescribed for amenorrhea (lack of a regular menstrual cycle); however they do not have any impact on bone mineral density loss and their continued use to treat amenorrhea is a sign of the research chasm at work.[33,34] Hormone replacement therapy for both men and women (obviously sex-specific hormones) is prescribed to address the symptoms of sexual disinterest or dysfunction and sexual organ atrophy. Various drugs to induce ovulation or generate increased fertility are prescribed for women and men with active eating disorders who wish to start families. Very rarely will a reproductive specialist recommend that a patient wishing to have a child attend first to weight restoration to improve fertility.

Pharmaceutical drugs used to reverse bone mineral density loss due to cumulative energy deficits from restricting food intake or insufficient food intake relative to energy expenditures are not prescribed to younger patients because they have very serious risks and side effects associated with long term use. The class of drugs is called bisphosphonates and these drugs stimulate osteoblast precursors[35] (cells associated with bone growth) and inhibit reabsorption of bone by osteoclasts[36] (cells associated with bone mineral reabsorption).

For younger patients, supplementation with calcium and vitamin D is often prescribed to address bone mineral density loss. A comprehensive meta-analysis on the use of calcium and vitamin D to prevent fractures associated with bone loss indicated that calcium doses of 1200 mg and vitamin D doses of 800 IU realized a 12% reduction in fractures of all types. But that is a relative risk reduction, so we have to look at the actual data to understand what that means. The median age for the women involved in these studies was 68 years of age. The median baseline risk for a fracture was 16%. Out of the 63,897 women studied, had none received any supplementation, 10,223 women would experience a fracture during the study time frames reviewed. A 12% relative reduction in fractures of all types means just shy of 2 women would not experience fractures out of those 10,223 women, if they were taking vitamin D and calcium supplements. And even when we extract specific studies within that meta-analysis that suggest a 24% relative risk reduction could be realized with improved compliance and reduced drop-out rates, that still only translates into only 4 women out of the 10,223 who avoid a fracture.[37] I'll go into some more detail on clinical trial assessment at the end of this chapter to help you become your own best advocate for your health outcomes.

Dr. Cheryl Rock and her colleagues at University of California, San Diego, investigate the associations between nutritional status and the risk factors and progression of various chronic illnesses:

Abnormal nutritional findings in patients with anorexia nervosa are primarily a consequence of semistarvation. Neuroendocrine abnormalities, degree of recovery, and phase of treatment affect interpretation of data.[38]

Their findings confirm that drug intervention for symptom management associated with ongoing restriction of food intake should not be confused with treatment of the underlying causative condition (i.e. an eating disorder).

There are drugs used to address neuropathies as well. Neuropathy, when present due to an eating disorder, occurs throughout the central, peripheral and enteric nervous systems and it's primarily associated with the demyelination of nerves directly attributable to energy deficiencies within the body. Unlike demyelinating diseases such as leprosy or multiple sclerosis, or damage due to chemotherapy or alcohol consumption, the demyelination that occurs with an eating disorder is largely reversible with rest and re-feeding. Symptoms of neuropathy, or nerve damage, range from numbness, tingling, itching, burning, aching, and sharp searing or electric pains. And such nerve damage also affects muscle control (both involuntary and voluntary).

Antiseizure medications (antileptics) for epilepsy are used off-label to treat neuropathies. Antipsychotic medications (neuroleptics) may also be prescribed, and tricyclic antidepressants are also prescribed off-label for neuropathies. These classes of drugs are all prescribed for their ability to suppress nervous system function.

Opioids are another class of drug often used for neuropathies. Unlike the neuroleptics and antileptics, opioids do not alter pain threshold or nerve transduction; rather they change the way the pain is perceived.[39]

Dr. Jane Ballantyne, professor emeritus at University of Washington, is an anesthesiologist and pain medicine specialist interested in promoting meaningful pain therapy:

Drug regulations certainly do not make it easy to provide opioid therapy for pain in a manner unfettered by prejudice and fear. Patients fear addiction—a fear that has been compounded by the criminalization of addiction brought about by drug laws. Physicians fear both causing addiction in their patients, and being punished for prescribing. Yet it is important to keep the risks of addiction and prosecution in proportion, to understand that both carry extremely small risk, and that they must be weighed against the devastating effect of chronic uncontrolled pain.[40]

Nonsteroidal anti-inflammatory drugs (NSAIDs) will often be prescribed when the patient is dealing with skeletal and/or connective tissue aches. For some patients, commonly when the sacroiliac joint becomes inflamed during recovery, it might be necessary to consider localized injection of lidocaine or the botulinum toxin (Botox®) to provide temporary relief.

Numerous other drugs may be prescribed to address symptoms of cardiovascular damage, renal (kidney) damage, and liver damage, and that's why patients with active eating disorders are commonly taking well over a dozen prescribed drugs daily by their mid-40s to alleviate symptoms and attempt to maximize quality of life as much as possible.

The treatment of symptoms associated with ongoing energy depletion in the body is complex and progressive.

When a recovery effort to full remission is not feasible (keeping in mind that such status isn't permanent or irreversible) then it's important for a patient to be proactive in her harm reduction efforts to maximize her health and quality of life. In those cases, all the above classes of drugs are important facets of enhancing and sustaining quality of life. In addition, working with a counselor or therapist to constrain avoidance behaviors around food can help alleviate the necessity of needing such drugs to suppress symptoms associated with the progressive damage from energy depletion in the body.

Not all physicians will necessarily be aware of the long-term implications for a patient who appears to eat "healthily" and exercise conscientiously yet who has a long history of an unresolved eating disorder. That is why it's particularly helpful if you, as a patient, are comfortable bringing your doctor up to speed on the fact that you have indeed been managing an active set of restrictive eating behaviors and/or rigorous exercise regimes and that you are well aware that many of the symptoms you face are the result of ongoing energy depletion over the years.

Many patients with chronic conditions feel compelled to hide the fact that they are not managing their active conditions exactly to the letter of what is recommended. Doctors are as much a part of our culture as we are, so of course they can be moralistic about chronic conditions being entirely within the patient's control. And we already know that many will fire their "noncompliant" patients rather than agree to treat them within the space in which the patients are most comfortable.

With eating disorders, the risk is not that a doctor might be judgmental of a patient actively avoiding food, but rather she will be supportive and enabling. The prevalence of eating disorders within the health care practitioner communities is equal to and sometimes higher than what is found in the population at large.[41,42,43,44,45,46]

As a result, the chance that your avoidant and restrictive behaviors around food will be perceived as being of absolutely no relevance to your current symptoms of ill health is unfortunately unacceptably high at present. It's all the more reason for you as a patient to be the expert in the necessity of preemptive and palliative treatment when an eating disorder is active.

Prescriptions for psychological symptoms

Treating patients with active eating disorders for their symptoms of anxiety, depression, or obsessive-compulsive behaviors with the classes of drugs often used to treat these mental conditions will have far less valuable outcomes for either symptom alleviation or sustainment of quality of life, than drugs that treat physical symptoms.

If antidepressants really were just Smarties, and had no adverse effects...[a]ntidepressants are not inert, however. Like all active drugs they change the body in ways that we are not fully aware of, and can have rare and long-term consequences that do not show up readily in clinical trials. For that reason alone, we need to be sure that antidepressants really do have worthwhile effects. This is the latest research to suggest they do not.[47]

Dr. Joanna Moncrieff, quoted above, is one of several well-known psychiatrists who are deeply critical of the indiscriminate use of psychoactive drugs for the treatment mental illness. Moncrieff contends that all drugs used in psychiatric treatments are not condition-specific and that they all suppress brain function. Such suppression may be warranted in certain acute or severe cases. Moncrieff dismisses the disease-centered model used by the psychiatric field today in favor of the drug-centered model whereby a drug is prescribed precisely because it will induce an abnormal or altered state, and not because it rectifies or ameliorates aberrant brain function.[48]

No drug is benign. There will always be risks associated with taking any prescribed drug. In circumstances where the quality of life is severely reduced, then the relative risk of taking a prescription that might improve the quality of life is more than acceptable to the patient. I encourage all patients to be aware of the risks of any prescription in relation to the potential quality of life that might be improved by taking the drug.

In many cases patients will be informed that not taking a drug will lead to unacceptable health risks. I will speak about how to understand those risks more clearly in the following section. When it comes to psychoactive drugs, patients are rarely informed of the risks associated with taking them and, in fact, little is known of their long-term risks in any case. In the absence of an acute or severe condition that may warrant the judicious and time-limited use of psychoactive drugs, it's wise to be extremely leery of starting on any so-called antidepressant, anxiolytic, or antipsychotic prescription. If, however, you are already taking these drugs, then it's equally important to be extremely conservative about quitting the prescription as well.¶

When you have an active eating disorder then most, if not all, of the psychological symptoms you face will be the direct result of energy depletion. Just as you should not be diagnosed with polycystic

---

¶ The process of tapering from a psychoactive prescription of any kind is an extended process. Never quit these prescriptions "cold turkey" and always seek medical oversight while you taper slowly off of the prescription(s) in question.

ovarian syndrome when you have an active eating disorder,[**],[49] it should be self-evident that you cannot be diagnosed with anxiety, depression, OCD, bipolar disorder, personality disorders, or psychosis when an active eating disorder is present. While an eating disorder is an anxiety disorder, getting the condition into remission isn't achieved through the application of any psychoactive drug.

Most importantly, we have ample evidence that restricting food intake and being in an energy-depleted state necessarily means that the psychoactive drugs are poorly absorbed, have a markedly reduced ability to induce an altered state for the patient, and do not improve rates of remission.[50,51,52]

Interpreting data

Humans can see faces in clouds. They can become physically nauseated at the thought of eating a type of food that happened to coincide with getting sick in the past. They can make snap judgments about everything and everyone, often in lifesaving ways and even more often in completely inaccurate ways.

In the absence of the practice of science, we depend completely upon our pattern sensing abilities. There are, in reality, no actual faces in those clouds. The reason you got sick was not that chicken dinner, but that someone with the flu sneezed near you three days before that chicken dinner. And the man you thought was planning on attacking you was actually racing to return those keys that you had failed to notice you had dropped.

[**] Polycystic ovaries are a common symptom of eating disorders and they resolve with re-feeding and weight restoration.

The practice of science is really an attempt at forcing our brains to work beyond pattern recognition as a way of trying to uncover the truth.

The data that is revealed through scientific inquiry isn't equal in relevance or applicability. Here is the hierarchy of data (from dodgiest to most indicative):

7. Survey questionnaire results, personal recollection, chatting with a friend

6. Case study

5. Epidemiological study

4. Randomized controlled trial

3. Single-blinded randomized controlled trial (RCT)

2. Double-blinded RCT

1. Systematic review and meta-analysis

Surveys and such

Human beings hold a lot of stock in firsthand or secondhand experience. If a friend tells you she's taken antidepressants and it's worked out swimmingly well for her, then you are going to weight that input as evidence of the value of considering taking antidepressants yourself.

If you were unable to heed the firsthand account of a friend who told you that a particular watering hole is crawling with crocodiles, then undoubtedly you would be risking your life. But whether your friend's experience with antidepressants is relevant to you or not requires that you apply the practice of science over your predilection to be drawn to such anecdotal evidence.

Science is a practice of inquiry that's set up to try to work around our brains' limitations and tendency toward biases that make us believe something is a fact when it's not. Human beings are fallible in their recollections, generally lack absolute reporting accuracy, and phrasing of the survey questions themselves can further skew the responses.

Surveys merely give us some starting points for further study.

Case studies

A case study is like being able to quiz your friend on her firsthand experience by speaking with her entire medical and/or psychiatric team and being able to sift through all her relevant test results and biomarkers. But the results that were achieved are not statistically relevant.

What does "statistically relevant" actually mean? Well, it can mean a bunch of things, but at its core it means that whatever is being looked at has not happened by chance.

Imagine you come across a case study of patient "M" who was successfully treated for an eating disorder by undergoing 12 sessions of acupuncture. There's enough clinical data to prove "M" was indeed in remission at the end of 12 acupuncture sessions. The problem is this result doesn't tell us whether her remission happened spontaneously, for other unknown or unmeasured reasons, or whether using acupuncture to realize remission from an eating disorder will turn out to be statistically relevant (meaning I could apply acupuncture to other patients and I will see remission more often than what I would expect to see by chance).

Epidemiology

Now let's imagine I take 10,000 people and I follow them in an epidemiological study over 35 years to try to figure out which diet appears to reduce the incidence of disease and death. These kinds of studies show us trends. For example, epidemiological studies show that a diet higher in fresh fruits and vegetables lowers risk of disease and death.

There are several issues with confusing the results of an epidemiological study with the causative results that can be achieved through controlled experimentation. First of all, despite the brilliance of epidemiologists, there is no way they can account for the myriad environmental inputs to ever suggest causation in any but the most blatant of outcomes.

I am a great fan of epidemiological studies as they are often the only way that ominous disease-generating factors can be uncovered in our environment. You have to start with uncovering correlations before you can get to what, if any, causative relationship might be present. Epidemiology uncovers correlation.

Does eating more fruits and vegetables lead to less illness and longer life? We don't know.

The only way we could know whether it really leads to less illness and longer life is if we had an experiment in which all other factors that could be influencing the outcomes of illness and death can be ruled out as influencers. Epidemiology studies things out in the world and not in the lab, and that means results can only provide indicators but not definitive outcomes.

We know that those in higher socioeconomic levels in our society have much greater access and the financial wherewithal to get and eat fresh fruits and vegetables. We know that those in lower socioeconomic levels of our society have greater rates of illness and lower life expectancies and they often have far less access to fresh fruits and vegetables as well.[53]

But would providing fresh fruits and vegetables to those of lower socioeconomic levels change their rates of illness and improve life expectancy? Everyone assumes so, but there's no evidence to back up that assumption.

It appears as though instigating urban community farms in low-income areas of a city is a great thing and provides very affordable access to fresh fruits and vegetables to those low socioeconomic levels of our society. But we have no data on whether it has any positive impact on morbidity and mortality rates. And if it did, is that result because involvement in community activity has allowed for individuals to experience the proven health-protective benefits of lowered isolation, or because veggies and fruits are part of their diet? Exactly.

Randomized controlled trials

How could we find out if eating fresh fruits and vegetables is so powerfully health protective that it overrides all other factors and inputs in an individual's life experience such that she realizes a much healthier and longer life no matter what?

We cannot.

In order to confirm whether the correlation of eating vegetables and fruit with longer, healthier lives is actually due to eating vegetables and fruit (and not some other unidentified and undetected factor), we have to apply a randomized controlled trial (RCT).

We do lifelong laboratory RCTs on animals, but when it comes to food experimentation we have a serious problem in extrapolating outcomes from mice, rats, or monkeys as being at all relevant to humans. We are the only creatures on the planet optimized to eat cooked food. That is a very important distinction. While we might be able to identify that rat stress and human stress are comparable, rats lack the 800,000-odd years' worth of evolutionary development to respond to that cooked food the way humans do.

The best way to figure out if, as an example, veganism confers any protective value on otherwise healthy human beings would be to do an RCT. We would take several hundred people and randomly place each in one of three groups: vegan, vegetarian, and control. By carefully screening upon entry into the study for preexisting conditions and disease, we could feel fairly confident that we could have them run out their lives and we would be able to determine whether veganism really does provide any statistically beneficial morbidity and mortality outcomes or not.

The problem is you cannot run a study like that. Veganism is a diet that is particularly difficult to adhere to (the vast majority are vegan for 1–3 years and 94% are ovo-lacto vegetarian after that point). Therefore most will not finish the study in such a way that we will have any data to crunch into some kind of statistical relevance. And never mind the fact that folks wouldn't be too keen to live in a laboratory for decades, either!

Studying the value that a diet has upon an existing diseased community is much easier. First of all, we don't need to run longitudinal studies (the benefits in symptom reversal will likely be noticeable within weeks) and we have a motivated community of participants.

In the end, RCTs (which can be single-blinded, double-blinded, or without blinding) are applied on humans with existing disease states and otherwise healthy controls for short periods of time as a way to at least determine if dietary changes can ameliorate a disease state or not.

If you are eating a gluten-free diet and you don't have celiac disease; if you are eating a vegan diet and don't have existing heart disease or rheumatoid arthritis; or if you are eating a low-protein diet and don't have kidney disease, then you aren't preventing illness or death; you are hastening it.[54] Reversing the impacts of an existing disease state has no proven relationship with possible prevention of the onset of those diseases.

Systematic review and meta-analysis

At the peak of the hierarchy of data is the systematic review and meta-analysis. These studies take the entire body of published research (and sometimes unpublished as well to circumvent publication bias) on a topic, assess the validity of inclusion or exclusion of each trial, and then examine the findings to arrive at a *fairly* definitive conclusion.

However, as I discuss in the paper "Part I: Systematic Review of Weight Gain Correlates in Literature," [55] fattism bias is so pervasive in scientific materials that the conclusions the authors offered in the review on sugar-sweetened beverage consumption and correlation with weight gain were not actually supported by the data they supplied within the published paper. Additionally, systematic review often can confirm correlations but cannot identify any underlying causes.

However, for patients who tend to latch onto mainstream articles that announce some definitive scientific finding about health and longevity, a great place to inoculate oneself against that kind of hype is the Cochrane Collaboration.[††] The Cochrane Collaboration gathers and summarizes the best evidence that is available from the research to date and at present it does so with no affiliations to interested industries or parties.

Still, once you've thoroughly investigated the limits of the research on the topic at hand, you will have to interpret its relevance in your specific case.

Risk vs. benefits of treatment recommendations

Let's say I have a chronic disease state such as heart failure. If I, as a patient, do not comply with non-pharmaceutical interventions (exercise, diet, fluid restriction, and weighing) then my hazard mortality ratio (HMR) is at maximum 1.57.[56] These numbers reflect data from subjects in a trial who did not comply with any non-pharmaceutical interventions for heart failure. As a refresher, an

---

†† http://www.cochrane.org/

SMR is the risk of death of a particular condition when compared to healthy human beings. HMR is the relative risk of dying within a group experiencing the same condition or disease under investigation.

My doctor might say to me, "But Gwyneth, you have a 60% increased risk of dying if you don't comply with my treatment recommendations!"

There are 191 deaths from heart failure per 100,000 people in the United States today.[57] That's (rounding up) 2 in 1000 people, or 0.2 in 100 people. By failing to comply with my doctor's non-pharmaceutical treatment recommendations, I have upped my actual mortality risk to 0.32 in 100 people.

I have a 99.8% chance of not dying if I follow my doctor's advice and I have a 99.68% chance of not dying if I don't follow my doctor's advice.

The relative risk is 60% (sounds scary) yet the actual risk is 0.12% (sounds silly).

And if I happened to be a patient where applying exercise, food and fluid restriction, and weighing regimes would activate an eating disorder, then my risk of dying due to an active eating disorder absolutely flattens the almost negligible reduction in risk of death associated with the outcomes of my heart failure.

And just so we are really, really clear here: heart failure is a chronic disease state. Inflammation is a risk factor for chronic disease. Treating risk factors has even less demonstrably valuable outcomes than treating disease states and that's because many with risk factors for disease will never develop the disease state in their lifetimes no matter their lifestyle, behaviors, or genetic predispositions.

You have between a 1 in 4 to 1 in 5 chance of dying due to an eating disorder if it remains active for twenty years. Very few chronic disease states will come anywhere near that mortality rate, with most sitting several decimal columns to the right of the decimal point in terms of risk.

But just because you cannot entertain our culture's one-note solution of diet and exercise to all the ills of the world doesn't mean that you cannot attend to many stress-based inputs that may be within your control. Your intimate relationships, your friendships, where you live and work, your opportunity to be able to sit in nature, your sleep, your sense of purpose and meaning, and your ability to be closely aligned with those things...these are all areas that can contribute to healing.

Personal, social, environmental, and economic factors in your life determine your health status and outcomes to varying degrees. These factors are all referred to as health determinants in public health policymaking. In recent years, the impact of income inequality as a health determinant has dwarfed other health determinants in its causal relationship to negative morbidity and mortality outcomes.[58] This means that by far the most impactful health determinant in your life is often outside your sphere of influence and attending to diet and exercise (personal factors determining health status and outcomes) will not remediate that impact.

Therefore it is also okay to be sick and stay sick. Because ultimately we may not have our health outcomes anywhere near our own control.

If you are concerned about the health implications of certain macronutrients, ultra-processed foods, remaining sedentary while in recovery, becoming "obese," and/or developing a chronic condition or disease state that you are told is the result of your food choices and activity behaviors, then viewing the cultural hype surrounding these topics with a very critical eye can help.

Ultimately, when you have an eating disorder, you must keep the following reality at the forefront of your understanding of the world as it relates to your best interests:

Eating disorder = deadly

versus

Various sundry chronic disease states = marginally deadly, somewhat quality of life inhibiting.

Socioeconomic health determinants = deadly

versus

Various sundry personal health determinants usually within everyone's locus of control = marginally improve quality of life in some cases if applied.

On the Eating Disorder Institute forums, I had the following analogy to offer up when those with a history of an eating disorder are contemplating (or have even been advised to follow) restrictive behaviors in the hopes that it will address chronic conditions that are distinct from symptoms associated with an eating disorder:

January 25, 2015 - Gwyneth

If you cannot eat unrestrictedly when hungry and rest when tired (as do non-ED people), then until you are doing everything in your power to model that non-ED behaviour, you are living the reality of an active eating disorder.

Bottom line is you don't get to play in the pseudoscientific sandbox of healthy living anymore. Only non-ED people are allowed to play there because it's just pretend for them and they don't actually follow through on living in the sandbox day and night because, well, it's actually full of cat dung and it's just a bit too gross to hang out in, if everyone's truthful about it all.

In fact, in fairly short order you'll realize that playing in that sandbox at all is just unsanitary and you'll start to pity anyone at all who thinks it makes sense to even play pretend in it, let alone live in it!

End Notes for Chapter Five

1. Alejandro R. Jadad, Alison Tonks, Carlos A. Rizo, Colin Guthrie, Dipan N. Mistry, Gabriel S. Gorin Rosenbaum, Julio Sotelo, Louise Ward, Magdeldin A. Elgizouli, Malcolm R. Macleod, Malvinder S. Parmar, Mark J. Wilson, Murray Enkin, Paul Root Wolpe, Peter Mc-Mullin, Robert I. Rudolph, and Valerie James, "What's a good doctor and how do you make one?" *BMJ (Clinical research ed.)* 325, no. 7366 (2002): 711-715.

2. Lawrence Dyche and Deborah Swiderski, "The Effect of Physician Solicitation Approaches on Ability to Identify Patient Concerns," *Journal of General Internal Medicine* 20, no. 3 (2005): 267-270.

3. Laurence H. Baker, Daniel O'Connell, and Frederic W. Platt, "'What Else?' Setting the Agenda for the Clinical Interview," *Annals of Internal Medicine* 143, no. 10 (2005): 766-770.

4. Gary Null, Carolyn Dean, Martin Feldman, and Debora Rasio, "Death by medicine," *Journal of Orthomolecular Medicine* 20, no. 1 (2005): 21-34.

5. Søren Holm, "What is wrong with compliance?" *Journal of Medical Ethics* 19, no. 2 (1993): 108-110.

6. *Basic Neurochemistry: Molecular, Cellular and Medical Aspects*, eds. Scott Brady, George Siegel, R. Wayne Albers and Donald Price (Cambridge, MA: Academic Press, 2005), 532.

7. Peter J. Norton and Esther C. Price, "A Meta-Analytic Review of Adult Cognitive-Behavioral Treatment Outcome Across the Anxiety Disorders," *The Journal of Nervous and Mental Disease* 195, no. 6 (2007): 521-531.

8. Scott N. Compton, John S. March, David Brent, Anne Marie Albano, V. Robin Weersing, and John Curry, "Cognitive-Behavioral Psychotherapy for Anxiety and Depressive Disorders in Children and Adolescents: An Evidence-Based Medicine Review," *Journal of the American Academy of Child & Adolescent Psychiatry* 43, no. 8 (2004): 930-959.

9. Stefan G. Hofmann, Anu Asnaani, Imke J. J. Vonk, Alice T. Sawyer, and Angela Fang, "The Efficacy of Cognitive Behavioral Therapy: A Review of Meta-analyses," *Cognitive Therapy & Research* 36, no. 5 (2012): 427-440.

10. Christopher G. Fairburn, Zafra Cooper, Helen A. Doll, Marianne E. O'Connor, Kristin Bohn, Deborah M. Hawker, Jackie A. Wales, and Robert L. Palmer, "Transdiagnostic Cognitive-Behavioral Therapy for Patients With Eating Disorders: A Two-Site Trial With 60-Week Follow-Up," *The American Journal of Psychiatry* 166, no. 3 (2009): 311-319.

11. Azy Barak, Liat Hen, Meyran Boniel-Nissim, and Na'ama Shapira, "A Comprehensive Review and a Meta-Analysis of the Effectiveness of Internet-Based Psychotherapeutic Interventions," *Journal of Technology in Human Services* 26, 2-4 (2008): 109-160.

12. Lise Gutknecht, Christian Jacob, Alexander Strobel, Claudia Kriegebaum, Johannes Müller, Yong Zeng, Christoph Markert, Andrea Escher, Jens Wendland, Andreas Reif , Rainald Mössner, Cornelius Gross, Burkhard Brocke, and Klaus-Peter Lesch, "Tryptophan hydroxylase-2 gene variation influences personality traits and disorders related to emotional dysregulation," *The International Journal of Neuropsychopharmacology* 10, no. 3 (2007): 309-320.

13. Margaret O'Dougherty Wright, Emily Crawford, and Darren Del Castillo, "Childhood Emotional Maltreatment and Later Psychological Distress Among College Students: The Mediating Role of Maladaptive Schemas," *Child Abuse & Neglect* 33, no. 1 (2009): 59-68.

14. Jungmeen Kim and Dante Cicchetti, "Longitudinal pathways linking child maltreatment, emotion regulation, peer relations, and psychopathology," *Journal of Child Psychology and Psychiatry* 51, no. 6 (2010): 706-716.

15. Robert M. Post and Susan R. B. Weiss, "Sensitization and kindling phenomena in mood, anxiety, and obsessive–compulsive disorders: the role of serotonergic mechanisms in illness progression," *Biological Psychiatry* 44, no. 3 (1998): 193-206.

16. Robert M. Post, "Kindling and sensitization as models for affective episode recurrence, cyclicity, and tolerance phenomena," *Neuroscience & Biobehavioral Reviews* 31, no. 6 (2007): 858-873.

17. Roel Verheul, Louise M.C. van den Bosch, Maarten W. J. Koeter, Maria A. J. De Ridder, Theo Stijnen, and Wim Van Den Brink, "Dialectical behaviour therapy for women with borderline personality disorder 12-month, randomised clinical trial in The Netherlands," *The British Journal of Psychiatry* 182, no. 2 (2003): 135-140.

18. Sören Kliem, Christoph Kröger, and Joachim Kosfelder, "Dialectical behavior therapy for borderline personality disorder: A meta-analysis using mixed-effects modeling," *Journal of Consulting and Clinical Psychology* 78, no. 6 (2010): 936-951.

19. Martin Bohus, Anne Sibilla Dyer, Kathlen Priebe, Antje Krüger, Nikolaus Kleindienst, Christian Schmahl, Inga Niedtfeld, and Regina Steil, "Dialectical Behaviour Therapy for Post-traumatic Stress Disorder after Childhood Sexual Abuse in Patients with and without Borderline Personality Disorder: A Randomised Controlled Trial," *Psychotherapy and Psychosomatics* 82, no. 4 (2013): 221-233.

20. Harriet Salbach-Andrae, Inga Bohnekamp, Ernst Pfeiffer, Ulrike Lehmkuhl, and Alec L. Miller, "Dialectical Behavior Therapy of Anorexia and Bulimia Nervosa Among Adolescents: A Case Series," *Cognitive and Behavioral Practice* 15, no. 4 (2008): 415-425.

21. Christoph Kröger, Ulrich Schweiger, Valerija Sipos, Sören Kliem, Ruediger Arnold, Tanja Schunert, and Hans Reinecker, "Dialectical behaviour therapy and an added cognitive behavioural treatment module for eating disorders in women with borderline personality disorder and anorexia nervosa or bulimia nervosa who failed to respond to previous treatments. An open trial with a 15-month follow-up," *Journal of Behavior Therapy and Experimental Psychiatry* 41, no. 4 (2010): 381-388.

22. Shireen L. Rizvi and Marsha M. Linehan, "Dialectical Behavior Therapy for Personality Disorders," *Current Psychiatry Reports* 3, no. 1 (2001): 64-69.

23. Ruth A. Baer, Sarah Fischer, and Debra B. Huss, "Mindfulness and Acceptance in the Treatment of Disordered Eating," *Journal of Rational-Emotive and Cognitive-Behavior Therapy* 23, no. 4 (2005): 281-300.

24. Marianne T. Marcus and Aleksandra Zgierska, "Mindfulness-based therapies for substance use disorders: Part 1," *Substance Abuse* 30, no. 4 (2009): 263-265.

25. Expwoman, "Part 1: History of Exposure Therapy for OCD: Dr. Victor Meyer and Ritual Prevention" *Exposing OCD* (blog), September 13, 2010, http://exposingocd.blogspot.ca/2010/09/part-1-history-of-exposure-therapy-for.html.

26. Karen Rowa, Martin M. Antony, and Richard P. Swinson , "Exposure and Response Prevention," in *Psychological treatment of obsessive-compulsive disorder: Fundamentals and beyond*, eds. Martin M. Antony, Christine Purdon, and Laura J. Summerfeldt (Washington, DC: American Psychological Association, 2007), 79-109.

27. Janet Treasure, "Motivational interviewing," *Advances in Psychiatric Treatment* 10, no. 5 (2004): 331-337.

28. Abdulbaghi Ahmad, Bo Larsson, and Viveka Sundelin-Wahlsten, "EMDR treatment for children with PTSD: Results of a randomized controlled trial," *Nordic Journal of Psychiatry* 61, no. 5 (2007): 349-354.

29. Bessel A. van der Kolk, Joseph Spinazzola, Margaret E. Blaustein, James W. Hopper, Elizabeth K. Hopper, Deborah L. Korn, and William B. Simpson, "A randomized clinical trial of eye movement desensitization and reprocessing (EMDR), fluoxetine, and pill placebo in the treatment of posttraumatic stress disorder: treatment effects and long-term maintenance," *Journal of Clinical Psychiatry* 68, no. 1 (2007): 37-46.

30. Andrea Bloomgarden and Rachel M. Calogero, "A randomized experimental test of the efficacy of EMDR treatment on negative body image in eating disorder inpatients," *Eating Disorders: The Journal of Treatment & Prevention* 16, no. 5 (2008): 418-427.

31. Wendy L. Waite and Mark D. Holder, "Assessment of the Emotional Freedom Technique," *The Scientific Review of Mental Health Practice* 2, no. 1 (2003): 1-10.

32. Hélène L. Gauchou, Ronald A. Rensink, and Sidney Fels, "Expression of nonconscious knowledge via ideomotor actions," *Consciousness and Cognition* 21, no. 2 (2012): 976-982.

33. Gary R. Strokosch, Andrew J. Friedman, Shu-Chen Wu, and Marc Kamin, "Effects of an Oral Contraceptive (Norgestimate/Ethinyl Estradiol) on Bone Mineral Density in Adolescent Females with Anorexia Nervosa: A Double-Blind, Placebo-Controlled Study," *Journal of Adolescent Health* 39, no. 6 (2006): 819-827.

34. J. D. Vescovi, S. A. Jamal, and M. J. De Souza, "Strategies to reverse bone loss in women with functional hypothalamic amenorrhea: a systematic review of the literature," *Osteoporosis International* 19, no. 4 (2008): 465-478.

35. N. Giuliani, M. Pedrazzoni, G. Negri, G. Passeri, M. Impicciatore, and G. Girasole, "Bisphosphonates stimulate formation of osteoblast precursors and mineralized nodules in murine and human bone marrow cultures in vitro and promote early osteoblastogenesis in young and aged mice in vivo," *Bone* 22, no. 5 (1998): 455-461.

36. D. E. Hughes, B. R. MacDonald, R. G. Russell, and M. Gowen, "Inhibition of osteoclast-like cell formation by bisphosphonates in long-term cultures of human bone marrow," *The Journal of Clinical Investigation* 83, no. 6 (1989): 1930.

37. Benjamin M. P. Tang, Guy D. Eslick, Caryl Nowson, Caroline Smith, and Alan Bensoussan, "Use of calcium or calcium in combination with vitamin D supplementation to prevent fractures and bone loss in people aged 50 years and older: a meta-analysis," *The Lancet* 370, no. 9588 (2007): 657-666.

38. Cheryl L. Rock and Joanne Curran-Celentano, "Nutritional disorder of anorexia nervosa: A review," *International Journal of Eating Disorders* 15, no. 2 (1994): 187-203.

39. Kristen E. Zorn and Jeffrey Fudin, "Treatment of Neuropathic Pain: The Role of Unique Opioid Agents," *Practical Pain Management* 11, no. 4 (2011): 26-33.

40. Jane C. Ballantyne, "Opioid analgesia: perspectives on right use and utility," *Pain Physician* 10, no. 3 (2007): 479-491.

41. A. Tülay Bağcı Bosi, Derya Çamur, and Çağatay Güler, "Prevalence of orthorexia nervosa in resident medical doctors in the faculty of medicine (Ankara, Turkey)," *Appetite* 49, no. 3 (2007): 661-666.

42. Tulin Fidan, Vildan Ertekin, Sedat Işikay, and Ismet Kırpınar, "Prevalence of orthorexia among medical students in Erzurum, Turkey," *Comprehensive Psychiatry* 51, no. 1 (2010): 49-54.

43. M. S. Alvarenga, M. C. T. Martins, K. S. C. J. Sato, S. V. A. Vargas, Sonia Tucunduva Philippi, and F. B. Scagliusi, "Orthorexia nervosa behavior in a sample of Brazilian dietitians assessed by the Portuguese version of ORTO-15," *Eating and Weight Disorders-Studies on Anorexia, Bulimia and Obesity* 17, no. 1 (2012): e29-e35.

44. Márta VargaEmail, Barna Konkolÿ Thege, Szilvia Dukay-Szabó, Ferenc Túry, and Eric F. van Furth, "When eating healthy is not healthy: orthorexia nervosa and its measurement with the ORTO-15 in Hungary," *BMC Psychiatry* 14, no. 1 (2014): 59-69.

45. Zali Yager, "Body Image Issues, Eating Disorders and Their Prevention in Male and Female College Students," in *Stress and Mental Health of College Students*, ed. Mery V. Landow and (Hauppauge, NY: Nova Science Publishers, 2006), 261-305.

46. Laura H. McArthur and Alan B. Howard, "Dietetics Majors' Weight-Reduction Beliefs, Behaviors, and Information Sources," *Journal of American College Health* 49, no. 4 (2001): 175-181.

47. Joanna Moncrieff, "Continuing the antidepressant debate: the clinical (ir)relevance of drug-placebo differences" *Joanna Moncrieff* (blog), July 2, 2014, http://joannamoncrieff.com/2014/07/02/continuing-the-antidepressant-debate-the-clinical-relevance-of-drug-placebo-differences.

48. Joanna Moncrieff, "Models of drug action" *Joanna Moncrieff* (blog), November 21, 2013, http://joannamoncrieff.com/2013/11/21/models-of-drug-action.

49. Janet, L. Treasure, E. A. King, P. A. L. Gordon, M. Wheeler, and G. F. M. Russell, "Cystic ovaries: A phase of anorexia nervosa," *The Lancet* 326, 8469-8470 (1985): 1379-1382.

50. Vassilis Martiadis, Eloisa Castaldo, Palmiero Monteleone, and Mario Maj, "The role of psychopharmacotherapy in the treatment of eating disorders," *Clinical Neuropsychiatry* 4, no. 2 (2007): 51-60.

51. J. E. Mitchell, M. de Zwaan, and J. L. Roerig, "Drug Therapy for Patients with Eating Disorders," *Current Drug Targets-CNS & Neurological Disorders* 2, no. 1 (2003): 17-29.

52. Carol B. Peterson and James E. Mitchell, "Psychosocial and pharmacological treatment of eating disorders: A review of research findings," *Journal of Clinical Psychology* 55, no. 6 (1999): 685-697.

53. Deja Hendrickson, Chery Smith, and Nicole Eikenberry, "Fruit and vegetable access in four low-income food deserts communities in Minnesota," *Agriculture and Human Values* 23, no. 3 (2006): 371-383.

54. Ashima K. Kant, Arthur Schatzkin, and Regina G. Ziegler, "Dietary diversity and subsequent cause-specific mortality in the NHANES I epidemiologic follow-up study," *Journal of the American College of Nutrition* 14, no. 3 (1995): 233-238.

55. Gwyneth Olwyn, "Part I: Systematic Review of Weight Gain Correlates in Literature" *Eating Disorder Institute* (paper), January 21, 2015, https://www.edinstitute.org/paper/2015/1/21/part-i-systematic-review-of-weight-gain-correlates-in-literature.

56. Martje H.L. van der Wal, Dirk J. van Veldhuisen, Nic J. G. M. Veeger, Frans H. Rutten, and Tiny Jaarsma, "Compliance with non-pharmacological recommendations and outcome in heart failure patients," *European Heart Journal* 31, no. 12 (2010): 1486-1493.

57. Division for Heart Disease and Stroke Prevention, "Heart Failure Fact Sheet," *Centers for Disease Control and Prevention*, last modified November 30, 2015, accessed January 1, 2016, http://www.cdc.gov/dhdsp/data_statistics/fact_sheets/fs_heart_failure.htm.

58. Kate E. Pickett and Richard G. Wilkinson, "Income inequality and health: A causal review," *Social Science & Medicine* 128 (2015): 316-326.

Chapter Six

Work, School, Family, Friends & Self

Food didn't kill people, for God's sake, people killed people. With their harping, and criticizing, and careful living. — Nina Killham

While it will be possible to reject as many toads as necessary to find appropriate professional support, you cannot completely sidestep the impacts and influences of colleagues, classmates, family, and friends.

This chapter takes a brief look at many day-to-day interactions and challenges you may face when adopting the Homeodynamic Recovery Method to get to remission.

Gwyneth: Where do you think you would be in your life now if you had not begun recovery?

Patient E: If I had not understood the damage I was doing to myself by restricting food groups constantly, tracking calories, working out all of the time while not nourishing myself enough, I'd no doubt still be following the latest trend in the diet world right now. I would be going through cabinets and throwing out perfectly good food in an effort to be "healthy" and "control" my weight and my chances for illness. I would be torturing my poor 3-year-old son by yelling at him for wanting to eat candy or cookies sometimes because they are "bad" foods and will most certainly kill him at a young age. I would be slaving over the stove for hours at a time trying to make everything from scratch while also raising a kid, taking care of my house, and being a wife while working part-time. I'd pretty much be running myself into the ground like I had been for the few years leading up to recovery.

Misplaced concern from the outset

When it comes to their commitment to pursue remission from an eating disorder, the vast majority of patients will receive initial support from family and friends. Although, if the patient is of average or above-average weight, there can be profound consternation regarding the necessity of pursuing recovery at all. Being told "but you look great!" will be a significant deterrent for any patient who is already trying to minimize the negative impacts of her avoidance of food.

If you are one of those unlucky enough to have family and friends that try to convince you that you are fine as you are, or, worse, actually believe that you should try to restrict your food intake further and exercise more because you are "overweight," then assigning some clear boundaries at the outset will ensure that your recovery process is protected.

For what it's worth, most patients with chronic conditions endure a lot of unsolicited advice from family and friends on how best to manage the conditions they face. And Western philosophies of individualism and positive thinking are limited in their ability to help us navigate the struggle of recovery while dealing with these kinds of difficult interactions.

The challenge with staunch individualism is it presumes mastery or failure will have no external inputs that make one outcome more likely than another. It denies the nature of human beings as social primates that cannot survive as individuals isolated from the group.

And while I can certainly argue that communal obligations in other cultures can be tremendously limiting and individually effacing, that is likely because I am a product of our Western individualistic culture myself.

We are each of us so deeply immersed in our culture that it's akin to the air we breathe—we struggle to imagine an alternate way of being. For example, consider this oft-repeated phrase: "Well, she has a right to her opinion and she has a right to state that opinion."

Does she?

In many societies around the world, while your thoughts may be your own, your right to verbalize them is not automatically allowed, let alone respected.

Consider the possibility that an unsolicited opinion does not automatically require that you accept the person's right to express it over your right to choose not to hear it. I'm not recommending that you become closed-minded, but rather that it's a reasonable approach, should someone insist you listen to her opinion, to ask her to reciprocate by listening to your opinion in return. Also, it is okay to state that opinions never need be re-stated once everyone agrees to disagree.

The second philosophy found in Western culture, positive thinking, has its roots in Calvinism* and it's a dominant way of living in the United States and hence much of developed world. What could be wrong with thinking positively?

Primarily positive thinking curtails critical assessment of the status quo. The status quo is accepted automatically as the ultimate and best solution. To question its validity is to become a negative thinker. Positive thinking presumes a just and fair world. If you follow all the rules and aren't a Negative Nelly, then you will be rewarded with health, happiness, and a long life.

When author Barbara Ehrenreich[1] was diagnosed with breast cancer and expressed her anger and frustration at having the condition with various online support communities, she received an intense stream of vitriol, fear, and hatred from other members of those communities. The positive-thinking consensus was that such negative feelings would ensure that she wouldn't survive her cancer. In other words, her negative stance would ensure an ultimately negative (and final) outcome.

---

* John Calvin (1505-1564) developed set of theological doctrines inspired by Augustine of Hippo. Calvinism, as it came to be known, includes the doctrine of predestination. Within the context of American history and culture, the tenet of predestination presumes that the poor deserve their poverty and the rich are realizing their manifest destiny. By the 19th century Calvinism was expanded by various influential thinkers of the day such that taking control of one's own destiny merely involved tapping into a powerful God who was no longer hostile or indifferent, but merely waiting to be called upon to realize best outcomes for the individual. Negative outcomes in one's life would henceforth be construed as a lack of faith or connection with God.

Optimism (positive thinking) and pessimism (negative thinking) are both rooted in fear and anxiety. They are two sides of the same coin. An optimist fears breaking the rule of accepting the status quo, as it ensures a bad outcome. A pessimist fears that entertaining the possibility of a positive outcome ensures that her hopes will be dashed.

A realist accepts that hopes may or may not be realized and that the world isn't always fair. If you suspect you are engaging with an optimist or pessimist when discussing the Homeodynamic Recovery Method, then anticipate that her worldview will not allow for measured consideration of things she fears too much to contemplate.

While you are likely going to read all the papers and posts on the Eating Disorder Institute website and this guide from cover to cover, it's unlikely that many family and friends will feel compelled to do so in order to understand fully both the process itself and the reality of what you must undertake in order to reach remission.

You don't have to explain your process to anyone if you don't want to. If you're a minor, you must work with your parents or guardians when it comes to your health care decisions. If you're an adult, then you may still feel a sense of obligation to work with family members to help them understand the rationale behind your decisions.

Cultural norms within almost all societies today dictate that your ability to adhere to an acceptable weight classification is a definitive marker of your social status and success. Unfortunately there is no easy way around that reality for all patients with eating disorders.

If your weight classification sits beyond culturally acceptable levels at any point in your recovery process, you will face tremendous pressure from others and commensurate insecurity in yourself.

Becoming adept at questioning the necessity of allowing the opinions of others to override your instincts, as well as discarding outright the validity of relegating a human being's worth to their outward appearance, will go a long way towards helping you reach remission from an eating disorder.

Awareness

In order to become more adept at interfacing with our dominant fattist culture while being true to your efforts to reach remission from an eating disorder, you have to make our automatic cultural frameworks available to your conscious scrutiny and critical assessment.

Exercise I

Spend two days keeping a notebook handy. Go about your usual activities involving interactions with family, friends, classmates, colleagues, etc.

Throughout the day whenever you get a spare moment, make a point of noting these interactions by describing the topics of conversation and the people involved.

If you found yourself paying attention to overheard conversations, take note of these interactions as well.

On day one, you are going to focus on identifying only the conversations that match the following criteria:

1) List the number of times that each person utters an "I should" statement. That doesn't necessarily mean they have to say the words "I" and "should," but rather that they are expressing their sense of having to follow through on something. They may use the words "must" or "ought to," or they may say "I plan to" but the nature of what is planned is an obligation of some sort.

2) List the number of times that each person speaks of their weight, shape, fat, or body parts, or is speaking of someone else's weight, shape, fat, or body parts. List whether the comment is negative, neutral, or positive.

3) Identify how many times a body statement (weight, shape, fat, or body parts) is subsequently linked to an "I should" statement.

4) Identify the number of conversations you may have had throughout your day (meaning not just exchanging a passing greeting) that had absolutely no examples of a body statement linked to an "I should" statement.

5) Rate your anxiety level (1 being relaxed and calm, and 5 being so agitated you may have to run from the room) for each one of these conversations in which you were involved (or overheard).

6) Rate your perceived sense of the person's anxiety level when he or she uttered both a body statement and the "I should" statement.

Exercise II

On day two, focus on each conversation that fits the following criteria:

1) List how many conversations involved a main topic that relayed the distress, crisis, or misery of individuals not known at all to the people present. Essentially these conversations usually reflect shocking news stories. Examples might include: a violent crime or accident where neither the victim(s) nor perpetrators are personally known to you or the others who are part of the conversation; natural disasters and wars; and fraud, cruelty, scams, and abuses of power.

2) List the number of times, during any of these conversations, anyone suggests any action that might be taken by those present to rectify the wrongs that have been highlighted in the news story being relayed. This list is usually very easy to complete—it almost never happens. An example might be: "I wonder if we could start an office donation to help those people who are now homeless because of that fire in the building across town?"

3) Rate your anxiety level (1 being relaxed and calm and 5 being so agitated you may have to run from the room) for each conversation in which you were involved. And also rate the overall mood of the group at the end of the conversation (where 1 is upbeat and relaxed, 3 is neutral, and 5 is down, stressed, and somewhat pessimistic).

For most of us, the results of this two-day experiment will not be surprising. Generally, you will notice that both *body + should* statements and news of distressing situations where there is no action that can be taken are anxiety-provoking conversations not just for you, but for everyone else around you as well.

It is not that we need happy and upbeat stories to alleviate anxiety, as such stories can also heighten anxiety as much as distressing stories. But rather we have to identify locus of control in a conscious way when we are exposed to today's global scope of uninterrupted inputs and interactions.

Loci of control

We all have an internal locus of control and an external locus of control: things that are in our control and things that are not.

Some events will never be in your locus of control, for example if your house is swept away by a freak mudslide. We can be somewhat prepared for events outside our control, a good example might be having house insurance, but many times there is no way to do anything except deal with the aftermath.

Western philosophies of life have generated a preponderance of assuming everything that happens to an individual resides within an internal locus of control. Got cancer? It's your fault because you should have exercised more, eaten better, slept more, been nicer to your kids. Your friend is injured in an accident? It's your fault because you should have told her not to go to that party—you had a sense it would turn out badly. Fired from your job? It's your fault because you had too many sick days, were rude to a colleague once, and never went golfing with your boss.

Of course living your life assuming everything is someone or something else's fault is equally unrealistic. Most life events are a combination of things we might have done differently to generate different outcomes and things that simply would have unfolded no matter our attempts to realize a different outcome. As Robert Sapolsky highlights in his book *Why Zebras Don't Get Ulcers*, the ability to identify when things are either inside or outside your locus of control mitigates your stress response enormously.[2]

Certainly, some things are clearly directed by an internal locus of control, and this is particularly the case if you are somewhere in a middle-class socioeconomic stratum in a developed nation. Decisions determining where you live, what food choices you make, where you go to school, where you work, the car you drive, and the clothes you wear all tend to sit within your internal locus of control. Your thoughts and feelings are largely, although not exclusively, within your internal locus of control as well. A clear example of when feelings are not entirely within your locus of control is as your threat response is activated in the presence of food. Other people's thoughts and feelings are most definitely not in your control.

Identifying your own locus of control may improve your interactions with others as you move through your recovery. Many people of faith embody that process in the serenity prayer:

God, grant me the serenity to accept the things I cannot change; the courage to change the things I can, and the wisdom to know the difference.

But faith is not required to identify internal and external loci of control.

Unfortunately, we often assume that our body is in our locus of control: we believe we should be able to say what weight it will be, how long recovery will take, how it will react to stress, and what pains we should or should not experience.

If we can accept that our minds exist within an ecosphere that, while supportive of the mind, is not actually controlled by the mind, then we can begin to understand the notion that the locus of control for our bodies is largely outside our conscious control.

It is wise to recognize that interfering with any ecosphere, including your own body, almost always involves some risk and may generate unwanted outcomes in the end as well.

The exercises outlined above and the concepts of loci of control will be merged in the next section so that you might practice identifying internal and external loci of control.

Body + should statements from others

First and foremost, you'll want to alleviate the anxiety you experience when you hear others speak of their diets, their horrible thighs, their self-admonishments for not going to the gym, or their refusal of a second piece of something tasty, because, unchecked, these things will run straight to the heart of your already eating disorder anxiety–heightened state. We commonly refer to these comments from others as "body shaming." Being mindful of the fact that the physical body falls almost entirely in an external locus of control will help frame how you proceed when others are body shaming.

When the topics turn towards *body* + *should* issues, then your primary goal is to keep their anxiety firmly in their locus of control. To achieve this goal, you have three choices in social circumstances (family, friends, colleagues, classmates, etc.):

1. Change the subject.

2. Wander away with some excuse of needing to go do something (if indeed an excuse is even needed).

3. Challenge it.

You have to be in a good space to feel the wash of anxiety that other people return to you when you challenge the status quo and unabashedly eat something offered with appreciation and gusto. You may note an obvious once up and down glance as they assess your body shape. And even worse there can be the retaliatory: "Oh, well you can afford to, but me I have to be careful!" or worse still there is the retaliatory "Really? You really think that's wise given, well…" (usually stated as they look you up and down or generate other non-verbal gestures that denote criticism and deny you your innate value as a human being).

In any case, if and when you are ready to take on a "challenge it" moment, then channel this quote from Erma Bombeck:

Seize the moment. Remember all those women on the Titanic who waved off the dessert cart.

No matter what choice you make, remember that their fear and anxiety is in their locus of control, not yours. A yawn is often contagious with many animals, but if you don't see it, you don't "catch" it. The same is true of all people's anxieties and the rampant body shaming you may encounter.

Even when you witness someone yawning, you are capable of suppressing the yawn in response when you are conscious of its contagion. The trick is to be conscious of the fact that anxiety is easily transferred from one person to the next, just like a yawn. If someone is worried about his or her diet, or exercise regime, or shape, then by consciously noting this is his or her worry you can halt the transfer of that worry to your own thoughts and feelings altogether.

Limit the background hum of arousal

The transfer of anxiety from your friend to you is much more likely to occur if you are already distracted and/or already dealing with a subconscious level of agitation and arousal. When you're in a relaxed state, your ability to maintain metacognition and boundaries is more solidly intact than when you are harried, distracted, and experiencing low-grade distress.

Interoception is the sense that we use to identify our internal physiological condition. And our ability to identify the arousal of our internal state varies depending on our cultural background. One study indicated that Europeans and Americans were more skilled at identifying an aroused internal physical state than East Asians.[3] Another study showed that Africans were more skilled at identifying an aroused internal physical state than Europeans.[4]

These studies were undertaken in laboratory settings and involved the subject's ability to perceive his or her own heartbeat. The ability to perceive a marked change in heartbeat (due to manipulation of stress stimuli in these experiments) is likely compromised in real-life settings, no matter the subject's cultural background.

Modern life emphasizes the need for multi-focusing and it likely places us in a cycle whereby we acclimatize to aroused states and perhaps preferentially pursue them in a way that is unavoidably tough on our bodies over the long term. Habitual multi-focusing may even lead us to a point where we experience a more relaxed state as an unpleasant and negative state to maintain.

Heightened arousal may put users in a "hunting" state, leading to rapid cycling (mentally, if not on the screen) through content and applications until arousal declines. In this state, the number of switches per minute increased, suggesting why so few seconds are spent per content segment. Once arousal has returned to preanticipatory levels, people may be less likely to switch while engaging with entertainment, work, or e-mail content. However, the effects of these content categories decrease as arousal increases and eventually leads to the next switch.[5]

The above assessment originates from a field study reviewing the way in which university students used their laptops during study sessions. And while younger generations switch focus more than older generations, the mental limitations of doing so are consistent across all generations.[6] We continue to multi-focus at work and at home despite the fact that it impairs our cognitive ability and has negative physical impacts as well.[7]

Drs. Zheng Wang and John Tchernev, of the Ohio State University School of Communication, uncovered that one of the reasons we persist with media multi-focusing or switch focusing despite its known impact of overall cognitive impairment, is that is provides unsought emotional gratification:

Consistent with the laboratory research, cognitive needs are not satisfied by media multitasking even though they drive media multitasking in the first place. Instead, emotional gratifications are obtained despite not being actively sought.[8]

It places us in a loop of "hunting" that creates short-term emotional rewards at the expense of long-term cognitive function and physical health. It takes conscious effort to readjust to feeling comfortable with a lower state of arousal, but the benefits of practicing to disconnect from these behaviors and unrelenting exposure to media will be that you can maintain effective boundaries throughout your recovery process.

Limiting exposure to all media outlets is also necessary because fattism is pervasive and heavily reinforced in those arenas. While fat phobia isn't an inherent facet of the expression of an eating disorder, we know that it's currently a dominant facet of how the condition is framed in today's culture.

Someone with severe asthma who wishes to become a diver has to come to terms with the fact that the risk to her life is significantly higher than for otherwise healthy divers. As someone with an eating disorder, if you wish to have a career as a classical dancer, a model, or an athlete, then know that the risk to your life is very severe when compared to otherwise healthy colleagues.

Individuals with chronic conditions can live their lives in defiance, acceptance, or denial of their conditions. Acceptance of a chronic condition is not a defeatist or acquiescent stance at all. If you decide you would like to pursue full remission and then you subsequently would like to protect that state, then acceptance will allow for you do that. Denying the real risk of relapse or defiantly insisting that such risks no longer exist and that you are "normal" are not protective approaches for maintaining remission.

It's about them and not you

It's probably a good idea to note at this point that professionals can be just as guilty of boundary invasion as family, friends, classmates, or colleagues. Not every statement that a professional makes to you will be an assessment or piece of advice originating from his or her professional expertise.

As mentioned in chapter 5 in reference to the bell-shaped curve of competence, a professional can be incompetent in his or her field of practice. However, even a professional of average competence will utter personal observations to a client or patient. It's important that you are able to differentiate between a clinical observation and a pronouncement is merely personal bias usually reflecting cultural norms. For example, if your therapist suggests you should eat less sugar, then that statement doesn't reflect professional expertise. With few exceptions, accredited therapists are not dieticians and therefore cannot offer nutritional or dietary advice in any professional sense. If you are unsure as to whether the advice you receive from your hired professional is a clinical recommendation or personal bias, then just ask for clarification. Alternatively, revisit chapter 5 and the section "Interpreting data" as a way of determining whether the advice you are getting is based on anecdotal or clinical evidence.

Generally the urge expressed by friends, family, classmates, and colleagues—in fact even strangers on the street—to comment on your recovery process reflects their needs and insecurities and not yours.

Sometimes inquiries will come from a place of genuine curiosity, concern, and interest, but more commonly they will be projections of the other person's own anxieties and concerns.

When asked a question such as: "But aren't you afraid of getting fat if you keep eating like this?" you may struggle to identify whether that question is about you or them. In cases like these, respond with a question such as: "Is that something you're worried about for me?" If the individual is genuinely interested in the process of what your recovery entails, then her answer will likely be, "No, I just wonder how you're approaching all of it given that I know you've been worried about that in the past," or something along those lines.

More commonly, broaching such a topic with you is an indicator of pervasive fattism. Such fattism originates with their internal biases and anxieties and has nothing to do with you. Answers like "No, but I mean you can't just keep eating and eating, right?" or anything that tends to start with "No, but…" will give you ample warning that the question reflects their drive to express their bias and anxiety and not to seek out your genuine response.

The sooner you can consciously register that the interaction is all about their anxieties, the sooner you can neutralize any further interaction on the topic. If you want to make it your job to help others stop being afraid of fat, then by all means engage with them further on the topic. But you have no obligation to do so.

"Well, that's not actually something I want to discuss with you. It's private," is one of many appropriate responses. Your body is your business.

Intellorexia

Of course, we would all love to be capable of protecting our own boundaries without harming others or ourselves, but the reality is that pursuing remission from an eating disorder in a fattist society leads to understandable bouts of genuine doubt and uncertainty. While you may find yourself outwardly managing to navigate the concerns of friends and family, inwardly you may be wracked with insecurities that only seem to mount as you move further along in your recovery process.

As a shortcut description of the cluster of thoughts and behaviors that can occur for many patients during the recovery process I coined the term "intellorexia" in a post in 2013. It is not a genuine condition of any kind, but rather a combination of anxiety and hyperintellectualism that is common for those in recovery.

Hyperintellectualism is a fairly self-explanatory term. Someone who is hyperintellectual is exceedingly drawn to complex forms of knowledge, philosophical matters, and efforts of intense conscious thought and rumination. While not all hyperintellectual individuals are anxious people, those who are quickly develop neural patterns that interweave the environmental-scan behaviors of the threat response with the conscious mind's predilection for intellectual minutiae.

This so-called intellorexia may be responsible for a patient failing to embark on recovery. But it might also be responsible for a patient failing to enter remission.

Intellorexia convinces you that there's always one more critical piece of information out there somewhere. Either it's something that will make recovery so compelling it cannot be resisted, or it's something that efficiently unlocks the one thing that isn't going right in your recovery such that you slide into that full remission without further complication.

If you find yourself mulling over a comment made by a family member or friend about your weight, or food intake, or the level of unhappiness and distress that they feel you express, then you will likely want to eliminate those doubts now planted in your mind by accessing more hard data.

In the early contemplative stages before embarking on a recovery effort, it's normal to seek out as much hard data as is available. But there are diminishing returns to seeking out increasing amounts of data once you've made the decision to begin recovery. And even that initial decision is never made from a space of absolute knowing. All patients have to make that decisive leap in the absence of absolutely knowing the outcome.

At some point during your recovery effort, you will have to change direction. You will need to stop looking for further information to bolster your commitment and instead stay the course by adopting behaviors that reinforce your commitment.

If you don't know a single soul who is accepting of his or her shape and size, then go out and meet some. You can start by becoming active in groups such as Size Diversity and Health, or Health at Every Size.[9] But also review what Ragen Chastain has to say in "What's the Deal with Healthy Lifestyle?"[10] on her website *Dances With Fat*, where she discusses falling into the trap of believing health is something that must be part of your innate value as a human being.

Start researching what it's like to refuse to watch or read anything weight/diet/health-related at all. Yes, this isn't an easy task in our world today but there really are some people out there who are engaged in other hobbies and pursuits. Really.

And if you're hyperintellectual by design, then disentangle that predilection from its enslavement to anxiety. There's too much to know and life is too short, so do you really want the sum total of your expertise to remain entirely rooted in eating disorders alone?

End Notes for Chapter Six

1. Barbara Ehrenreich, *Bright-sided: How Positive Thinking Is Undermining America* (New York: Metropolitan Books, 2010), 25-26.

2. Robert M. Sapolsky, *Why Zebras Don't Get Ulcers,* Third Edition (New York: Henry Holt and Company, 2004).

3. Christine Ma-Kellams, Jim Blascovich, and Cade McCall, "Culture and the body: East–West differences in visceral perception," *Journal of Personality and Social Psychology* 102, no. 4 (2012): 718-728.

4. Yulia E. Chentsova-Dutton and Vivian Dzokoto, "Listen to your heart: The cultural shaping of interoceptive awareness and accuracy," *Emotion* 14, no. 4 (2014): 666-678.

5. Leo Yeykelis, James J. Cummings, and Byron Reeves, "Multitasking on a Single Device: Arousal and the Frequency, Anticipation, and Prediction of Switching Between Media Content on a Computer," *Journal of Communication* 64, no. 1 (2014): 167-192.

6. Ibid.

7. Mark A. Wetherell and Kirsty Carter, "The Multitasking Framework: The Effects of Increasing Workload on Acute Psychobiological Stress Reactivity," *Stress and Health* 30, no. 2 (2014): 103-109.

8. Zheng Wang and John M. Tchernev, "The "Myth" of Media Multitasking: Reciprocal Dynamics of Media Multitasking, Personal Needs, and Gratifications," *Journal of Communication* 62, no. 3 (2012): 493-513.

9. "About ASDAH, HAES®," *Association for Size Diversity and Health*, accessed January 1, 2015, https://www.sizediversityandhealth.org/about.asp.

10. Ragen Chastain, "What's the Deal with Healthy Lifestyle?" *Dances With Fat* (blog), October 17, 2012, http://danceswithfat.wordpress.com/2012/10/17/whats-the-deal-with-healthy-lifestyle.

Chapter Seven

When the Norm Isn't Normal

May 13, 2012 - Freckled Bean

I have two grandmas: one who announced that I was getting a "huge belly" at 13 years old and praised me during the holidays on how healthy I looked at BMI [emaciated] and one who, during this same holiday when I was BMI [emaciated], burst into tears as soon as I left the room because of how thin I was. Now when I see her she has to squeeze my newly cushy hips and tell me I look great a hundred times.[*]

One dilemma a patient faces when determining that applying the Homeodynamic Recovery Method for pursuing remission from an eating disorder is suitable for them, is that they may very well get fat. Or, more accurately, the adipose (fat) organ will need to enlarge beyond its inherited optimal size for a number of reasons that are understood when it comes to restoration from restriction, and for many more reasons that are not yet fully understood.

---

[*] Eating Disorder Institute forum post.

For legions of individuals with eating disorders (and also those without, too), the possibility that remission may include fatness will make the Homeodynamic Recovery Method seem unacceptable—in fact, not just unacceptable, but irresponsible.

Philosophy of the Homeodynamic Recovery Method

As I mentioned at the introduction of this guide, there's little within the scope of this method for reaching remission that cannot be found in every other science-based program currently available. The re-feeding guidelines, the requirement to cease exercise and rest, and the involved guidance of medical support and a suitable therapist to retrain the mind to practice non-avoidant behaviors around food, are all standard science-based recovery program fare.

However, the norm in our society is to accept the following falsehoods as true: a) obesity has a causative role in the onset and progression of numerous chronic conditions; b) fat is an energy storage unit rather than the actual highly sensitive metabolic manager that it is; and c) diets (restricting food intake or food groups) and exercise are necessary to "treat" the presence of an above-average sized fat organ to realize presumed improvements in morbidity and mortality outcomes.

The Homeodynamic Recovery Method accepts the following evidence-based confirmations as true: a) obesity has no proven causative role in the onset of any chronic condition[1,2] and its appearance may be a protective response to the onset of numerous chronic conditions generated from currently unknown cause(s);[3,4,5,6] b) the fat organ is the largest hormone-producing organ in the body and it produces hormones that gate critical body functions as diverse as bone and blood formation and reproductive and metabolic functions;[7] and c) diet and exercise regimes are hyped beyond all proportion regarding their actual scientific value for health and longevity in human beings.[8,9,10,11] let alone being viable treatments for reducing the size of a critical hormone-producing organ in the body. The fat organ should no more be reduced in size than the kidneys should be reduced in size.

Furthermore, fatness exists within our populations naturally. It is merely the outlying standard deviation from average weight. A human being can be naturally above-average weight, just as a human being can be naturally above-average height. Both height and weight are highly heritable (genetically transmitted) traits.

Obesity that appears in an individual who doesn't have the inherited genetic predisposition to be fat isn't the result of poor diet and lack of activity. As best as researchers have been able to determine at present, the fat organ enlarges beyond its inherited size in response to environmental stressors affecting the body: sleep deprivation, exposure to endocrine disruptors in the environment, unrelenting stress (highly correlated with income inequality), and perhaps many more as yet uninvestigated triggers.

Further clinical data is available on the Eating Disorder Institute site in the papers categorized under obesity concerning fat organ size and enlargement. Within the context of the common temporary fat mass enlargement associated with recovery from an eating disorder, please refer back to chapter 3.

As it's normal to be endlessly fat-shaming self and others in conversation; chatting and boasting about exercise regimes and workout sessions; and forever recommitting to "eating healthy" for the New Year, for Spring, for the Beach Body, for Going Back to School, then being someone who has navigated an eating disorder into remission can sometimes make you feel as if you are in a sci-fi movie surrounded by pod people[†] or synths.[‡]

These sociocultural influences are one of many major triggers for relapse for those either undergoing the recovery process, or those in remission. Here are some of the ways in which I've framed managing these challenges in responses on the Eating Disorder Institute forums in the past:

September 3, 2012 – Gwyneth

You don't need to be positive. You don't even need to be hopeful right now. You can be sad, frustrated, angry, disappointed and depressed. Negative emotions are not comfortable emotions, but they are not emotions to be banished or squashed with happy chipper facades.

The ones who push through to complete remission do not do it whistling a happy tune with a smile on their face. Anger, deep sadness and feelings of withdrawal and staying in the home are normal facets of recovery. Some things have to be stripped away to be properly rebuilt.

In our societies we assume that depression is brain dysfunction. In fact, it appears as though in many cases it's a biological function that allows for the brain to reduce outside inputs to allow for healing and the increased

---

† Reference to the 1955 novel The Body Snatchers [Scribner Paperback, New York, 1954] and the nickname given to the alien species that spawn replicas of the humans on earth.

‡ Reference to the American/British television series Humans [June 2015] where "synths" are androids made to look and behave like humans.

ability to think through and resolve very complex problems. The problem is one of transformation: Who are you now? Is what you see in the mirror the sum total of your existence, your potential, your purpose? You are meant to consider these tough questions and not try to wipe them out or assume that they are signs of the recovery process not working for you.

It is very akin to a grieving process. There is no way to short circuit a grieving process or somehow fast-forward it. You trudge through it.

You are grieving the entire thing—the loss of what might have been had you never had an eating disorder, the loss of nostalgically remembering feeling in control and strong when in the heart of the eating disorder (it was an ED-generated mirage, but you still likely felt that way at the time), the fear of the new and completely unknown you and what the future holds without ED—all of it is how you transform to your new resilient normal. I cannot really tell you to embrace the grief, because no one can really embrace the kick to the gut that grieving is, but you can mindfully move through it.

Be water.

"*Don't get set into one form, adapt it and build your own, and let it grow, be like water. Empty your mind, be formless, shapeless—like water. Now you put water in a cup, it becomes the cup; you put water into a bottle it becomes the bottle; you put it in a teapot it becomes the teapot. Now water can flow or it can crash. Be water, my friend.*"

Bruce Lee (believe it or not)

In a psychological sense, water can flow and it can provide enough buoyancy to hold up and support a huge freighter. In other words, let yourself hold a grief-stricken thought (water in the cup) and then let it flow through you like water through your fingers. Feel bad and then allow yourself to identify that you can also feel better—it will move back and forth throughout the day.

The seven signs of remission

Full remission from an eating disorder is perhaps a more enlightened and healthful state than the state in which many with no history of an eating disorder currently live. In a society rife with both healthism and fattism—meaning that people are discriminated against on the basis of being ill or fat—someone who has worked to get an eating disorder into full remission lives utterly beyond those prejudices. They know that hatred of any kind is harmful to one's physical and mental health. Thus there is heightened resilience to be had in remission.

Remission will ultimately be how you choose define it. But here are seven features that I've found help frame how remission is lived and experienced:

1) You look forward to gatherings and celebrations that center on food. Like all those without an eating disorder, you indulge happily and do not compensate either before or after the event.

2) You have no forbidden foods, unless of course they could actually kill you (e.g., peanut allergy).

3) You are a force for moral absolution. Your relationship with food is a morality-free zone and it has far-reaching influence on those around you, not to mention yourself.

4) You experience your body, and every body, as a miracle every day. You marvel at the healing of a bruise. You stop to watch your fingers flying over a keyboard and are amazed. You see form and function and the innate power of the body.

5) You understand on a cellular level that "savoring" is a state of transcendence and transubstantiation. Transforming food into life-giving energy is phenomenal!

6) You feel connected. While many with eating disorders can feel strangely energized and alive in a state of extreme energy depletion, they rarely feel connected in that state. In fact, they feel a high in the disconnection. Connection is actually an ambivalent state and you are able to hold the ambivalence with appreciation. It is not always joyous, supportive, or healing to be connected to others. But you are ok with that.

7) You are fluid (see the above quote from Bruce Lee for an explanation).

Relapses

Gwyneth: When you lapsed, what did you learn from those lapses and how did they change how you practiced recovery behaviors once you returned to a recovery effort?

Patient N: I learned how terrifyingly quickly the ED noise can swoop back in, and how it's not simply a matter of pushing the door shut again. I learned that I really needed to do some serious mental work if I was ever to reach remission—I started mindfulness practice and I started to journal pretty much daily, a process which helped enormously. But also, I learned that I couldn't rush myself through recovery, and that although

I felt isolated and uncertain for a really long time, perhaps I needed that time for the real seeds of remission to germinate. I also came to feel almost thankful that my body happened to change so very much and so quickly, in terms of weight and swelling, because it really forced me to face my fears about gaining weight head-on. There was no going back, and so I had no choice but to work on acceptance and surrender.

Patient P: One shock I got was last December. I caught a nasty virus that laid me low for about 3 weeks. During that time I was quite ill and could only manage 2000-2500 cals per day, compared to 3500-4500 normally. Once I got better I assumed that it would be a simple case of just picking up food and eating it. But the 3 weeks of low intake was enough to make eating more very difficult. It took at least a month to get comfortably back to normal amounts of food. My appetite came roaring back, but my ability to respond to it was impaired. I can see now how tough relapses are and just how quickly things can get out of hand.

Relapses aren't failures. They're the norm, not the exception. A relapse offers the potential for a more resilient remission down the line. It doesn't matter how many slips or lapses occur, remission is as feasible whether you have experienced one slip in a decade or dozens of lapses in a single year.

Those with rheumatoid arthritis cannot always live their lives keeping the condition in remission—too much stress, too many deadlines, not enough sleep, no regular meals...things happen. And does someone with rheumatoid arthritis sense a flare coming on? Yes. Are they pretty depressed when the flare happens and they're stuck having to work it back into remission? Yes. But they don't additionally beat themselves up for the fact that these things happen, and they simply restart the process of taking care of themselves in the ways that will hasten a remission.

And unlike arthritic flares, a flare of an eating disorder involves brain impairment. And so, just as you plan a safe option for getting home before you head out to a party where you'll be drinking, you need to plan your relapse reversal intervention *before* it happens.

Relapse reversal intervention kit

If you have a few bad days where you find yourself restricting food intake, or over-exercising, or purging, then now is the time to pull out your relapse reversal intervention kit. What you include in your kit is dependent on your individual needs, but generally you'll want to cover the following facets:

- Go back to a safe meal plan that ensures you are eating to the minimum intake guidelines. Use your safe meal plan even if you think it's not necessary. Your body is and will always be very sensitive to any slight energy deficit and the easiest way to reverse that pull toward increasing the restriction is to stop it dead in its tracks.

- Identify the triggers that pulled you into restrictive behaviors. Then develop a plan to lessen, avoid, remove, or otherwise neutralize these triggers once you've identified them.

- Accept the fact that you have a new normal. Some things that are fine for others will never be fine for you. Fashion magazines may be fine for your friends, but are simply too triggering for you. Likewise, those with alcohol dependence tend to protect their sobriety by not working in a bar.

- Don't hesitate. See your trusted advisors for tune-ups: doctors, therapists, dieticians. Asking for help isn't a marker of failure; it's the opposite.

Your relapse reversal intervention kit will contain a list of things you need to do as soon as you identify there has been a slip. It's your commitment to yourself to treat restrictive eating behaviors as a condition that occasionally flares and requires remedial action to bring it back to complete remission.

Consider making the kit a tangible thing. Purchase or make a box and keep it by your bedside. Put the phone numbers of your therapist, doctor, a good supportive friend and family (if they're not nearby). You'll likely have kept a journal during a portion, if not all, of your recovery process. Put that journal in the box. Also add a spare blank journal ready to use to get back on track. There is a Recovery Journal available through the Eating Disorder Institute website, but any journal will do.

Write and include a letter to your future slipping or lapsing self with reminders of all the reasons why remission is valuable for you and to you. Place any mementos or inspirational items there as well—anything from a player loaded with music that's meaningful to you, to a stuffed animal that comforts you (yes, you too, adults), to a fridge magnet with a saying that kept you going in recovery when it was pretty bleak.

Many find the recovery process so profoundly transformational that they decide to get a tattoo or purchase a piece of jewelry. Take a photo of that item and place a print of that photo in the kit. There are many recommended books to be found on the Eating Disorder Institute website under Resources (Books and Workbooks), so consider adding any of those you used during recovery to the kit as well.

And most importantly, before any slip occurs, write a To Do list that spells out precisely the steps you will follow to get back to full remission and place that list at the top of the kit. Make the first step the requirement of telling someone suitable that you've slipped—and not someone you know only in an online setting. Accountability is an important facet of returning to the practice of remission.

Common causes of relapse

The causes listed here are by no means comprehensive, but they will offer several areas to be certain of covering off as you enter remission as way of protecting that remission indefinitely.

Energy deficits

Sensitivity to energy deficits is one of the most pernicious reasons that a slip will morph into a full-blown flare. If you're uncomfortable with reinforcing your need to eat at regular intervals, consider that many with other chronic conditions must do so and there is no need to feel you are putting others out. Those who suffer from migraines, hypoglycemia, diabetes mellitus, and various gastrointestinal conditions (just to name a few) have to maintain their energy balance in very conscious ways and so will you.

Have ready-to-eat snacks everywhere: your car, your purse, your coat pockets, and your desk at work. If you're liable to skip snacks and meals because you get busy, then set up your computer or mobile phone with alarms that remind you of the need to break to eat.

Both neuropeptide Y (NPY)[12] as well as dopamine-orexin[13] interactions have been implicated in the anomalous response of those with an eating disorder when the body needs more energy. There are even some intriguing new investigations in progress as to whether antibodies specific to these orexigenic (driving the need to eat) neuropeptides and neurotransmitters may play a causative role in that drive to keep moving and stop eating that marks an active eating disorder.[14] Generally it looks as though those with active eating disorders produce orexigenic neuropeptides and neurotransmitters as do healthy controls, but the response is anorectic (eat less/move more).

For some patients in remission, something as seemingly innocuous as fasting for a medical screening test will generate a sufficient energy deficit as to precipitate relapse. Some can be sensitive to a daily energy deficit as slight as 200 kcal.

By far the best way to avoid a slip is to pay attention to needing to eat regularly and consistently. If you have family or friends who can offer you reminders when you seem to be distracted, stressed, or just very busy, this will go a long way to keeping you well away from a spiral into full-blown relapse.

Career and activity choices

Many aspiring dancers, models, actors, fashion designers, and athletes contact me looking to find a way to "just get over" their eating disorder so that they might pursue their dream.

While I suspect that there are those in such professions who are truly successfully in remission, I have no direct experience with that outcome. I anticipate that this state is the rare exception to what I habitually see when a patient attempts to juggle the need to get to remission while immersed in these types of careers. These jobs are all exceedingly lean-focused career choices in today's fat-phobic world.

Two chiropractors, Drs. Cesar Hincapié and J David Cassidy, conducted a systematic review to isolate menstrual disturbances and low bone density in professional dancers, and extracted the following results:

The lifetime prevalence of any eating disorder was 50% in professional dancers, while the point prevalence ranged between 13.6% and 26.5% in young student dancers.[15]

Not surprisingly, the prevalence data for those in these fields who deal with active eating disorders is incomplete because revealing the condition might well end a career. Some evidence tentatively confirms greater prevalence of partial eating disorder and substance abuse rates in fashion models when compared to healthy controls.[16,17] What researchers have identified is that while the fashion models studies may not have met DSM criteria for eating disorders, they had significantly higher rates of disordered eating behaviors than healthy controls and they had alcohol dependency issues at almost three times the rate of healthy controls as well. The data on the prevalence of eating disorders in elite athlete communities is more solid and confirms a higher rate of eating disorders, amenorrhea (in women), and bone density loss when compared to healthy controls.[18,19]

Remission can only be solidly entrenched with consistent unrestricted eating behaviors and very careful application of activity that is not prone to being readily ratcheted up in frequency, duration, and intensity. In these lean-focused professions there is nothing within your day-to-day world that can support that need to protect your remission (let alone find a way to get to remission).

Sometimes things happen in our lives that require of us that we find a new path. I'm also cognizant of the fact that if you are an aspiring actor, dancer, or athlete with an active eating disorder, you'll likely reject my suggestion that your current professional aspirations are no longer in your best interests.

Pursuing harm reduction is most certainly a suitable option if you would prefer juggle these kinds of careers with an eating disorder. However harm reduction will only lessen the angle of the grade of deterioration—it does not halt the deterioration altogether. Most cases of those with active eating disorders in these professions quickly become too ill to realize even partial tangible success in their careers of choice. If you're hospitalized with an eating disorder–driven crisis, it's very likely you will miss that big career break more often than not.

What we do as our profession is not who we are as a person, nor is our profession foundational in any partnership or life plan. Even if you're a professional model, actor, athlete, or dancer, you're still not what you do. Nothing in your life should be indispensable or inherent to your self-definition as that's not a resilient approach to life. No matter what taken away from us, in the end we still have to be "us".

Remission of a deadly neurobiological condition such as an eating disorder takes precedence over clinging to need to define your value in the world by what you do. You have innate value because you exist.

If an eating disorder has gotten to the point where it needs intervention, then at the very least commit to being on hiatus from your professional efforts until you are in remission. And while you're in recovery, spend some time assessing who you are and what draws you to the career in question, and whether there are ways to be involved in the profession while protecting your remission. Work with a counselor or therapist to maintain your curiosity about what might be possible—one door may be closing, but take a look around and investigate what else is right there in your immediate surroundings.

Should you arrive at the decision, with the help and support of your counselor or therapist, that your professional goals and dreams are nonnegotiable, then you will need to thoroughly repurpose your twitchy threat identification system to be on sentinel duty for protecting your remission. In other words, instead of your threat identification system remaining latched onto misidentifying food as a threat, instead you are going to train it to keep you and your remission safe.

As mentioned in the previous section, you must create some discipline and rigidity around making sure you're sufficiently energized through both adequate and unrestricted food intake as well as careful attention to the risks of habitual activity pulling you toward restriction. Ideally, find a colleague or teammate who has no history of restrictive eating behaviors and use the buddy system whereby if she's eating, then you're eating. Maintain regular contact with your therapist or counselor and develop connections outside your career path that are decidedly not at all lean-focused.

Again, these suggestions do not necessarily offer the best path forward for protecting remission, but the reality is that few believe that their dreams for pursuing greatness in lean-focused careers are truly unattainable simply because an eating disorder is in the picture. And I cannot say with any certitude that that approach is wrong.

How partners, families, and relationships increase the risk of relapse

August 30, 2012 – clk

You are not alone in this. I, too, expected to have my husband's support when I first opened up to him about my eating disorder. Instead, he threatened to leave me and take my son if I didn't "stop." That was four years ago, and since then I have been in two outpatient programs, so obviously he did not mean that. But I truly think some people (men especially) are just not capable of dealing with conflict/distress/illness in a healthy way. When I was sick, he did not discuss it with me at all until it was obvious that I was very, very ill. Then he demanded that I go to treatment or I'd have to quit my job, etc.

As for some practical advice, make sure you are getting lots of support elsewhere. I have many friends I can be candid with about my ED, a fabulous therapist, and a dietitian. All of these people are willing to listen to me when I need it, without jumping in to try and minimize or fix the situation. Sure, it is disappointing that the one person I wish could support me through this is unable/unwilling, but that is just how it is.

November 27, 2012 - Iamsavingmyself

I posted about my mother here a few days ago and the more I think about her the more scared I get. She's definitely well under her natural weight and has been for decades, uses her gluten and lactose intolerance as an excuse to restrict, thinks she's "better" than others because she has "self control" and is thin and is essentially orthorexic. I grew up with plenty of comments like "you'd be happier thinner", "that's fattening", "you shouldn't sit down so much", "stop snacking", "you're a bottomless pit, stop eating" (none of these are the gist of what she said, they're all direct quotes). She actively judges people based on their weight and says TV actresses have gotten fat when they've only gone from skinny to slim. When my ED first started I realised what it was pretty quickly and threw myself into it (even looking at pro-ana nonsense) because I thought it would make me happy and it might finally make her feel like she had a good daughter.

May 13, 2012 - Vangirl

Ugh, so I am visiting my family and so far the week has been really great. I was really dreading this vacation because I have not seen my friends or family from home since Christmas and since then I have gained weight. Well, today we're having a BBQ…and I was really excited to catch up with my family. My grandma was the first to arrive. She's very old and is losing her memory a bit, but lo and behold she has not forgotten how to criticize because one of the first things she said to me was, "Are you pregnant?"…I am sitting in my mom's room crying. My sister and my mom have come in to chat with me and tell me how strong

I am and to also "consider the source" (my grandma is critical of everyone all the time, she has no filter, etc.). Of course, I know all this, but it does not make me feel any better. The belly is my sore spot. I am so conscious of it because I was adamantly teased about my belly when I was younger (a close friend of mine even wrote a poem about me, which was extremely mean). I just can't help but feel like that young girl again all insecure and self-conscious. Now I have to go out and chat with my family, but all I feel like doing is staying in my mom's room…I know I can't do that and will eventually have to come out. But I just didn't think I was still so sensitive about my body. It sucks!

July 4, 2012 - Orgeluse

How do you overcome being dependent on other people's opinion about food, their food-choices?!

I was planning to have pasta after work and some pizza in the evening. Now my BF suggested "just have a snack now and we can share the pizza this evening" – it screwed up all my plans, I felt guilty for planning to eat so much. I felt sad and angry, like someone had taken away the food from me. I can't eat at all now. I should just eat like I planned but I can't.

It's the same about portions sizes – I always want others to eat more than me, so I'll feel less guilty. I felt so relieved seeing my colleague snacking at work like it "allows" me to eat, too.

HOW CAN I OVERCOME THIS? Just one comment screws up my whole day. I was unkind to my bf, I am in a deep hole of sadness and my mind I think switched to "starvation mode" as the big hunger I felt after work has disappeared now and I don't want to eat and don't know what to eat :-(

Many of the experiences above reflect just a few of the ways in which a recovery process may end up uncovering relationship issues and challenges navigating social situations that have been evaded and buried through using restrictive behaviors.

As recommended by the Eating Disorder Institute forum member "*clk*," involve your treatment team and, in particular, your therapist or counselor in helping you to navigate the entire non–eating disordered (and eating disordered) world around you, both while you work through recovery and periodically in remission as well.

In my firsthand and therefore certainly not statistically significant experience, patients who remain with unsupportive and difficult partners often struggle to get to remission and appear to have more severe and prolonged symptoms throughout the recovery process, although I have seen several exceptions as well. There have been a number of patients with unsupportive partners who have remained with the partners and yet reached a fairly straightforward and resilient remission within two years; and there have been patients with very supportive partners where the recovery process has been protracted and difficult over four years or longer.

Financial dependence appears to have a tremendously stressful impact on the one attempting recovery if she (or he) is with an unsupportive partner. In those cases, therapy seems to have offered excellent levels of inoculation over time against that level of stress such that recovery can continue to full remission.

There is no one-size-fits-all answer for navigating the drive to relapse when pressures are directly placed on you by loved ones—the term used in psychotherapy is "countermoves" or "change backs." Dr. Murray Bowen developed the Bowen family systems theory in the

1950s in which, among many other facets of family interactions, he identified that, when one family member attempts to develop a more independent self, there are a series of countermoves by other family members to push for a return to the status quo.[20]

As Dr. Harriet Lerner explains, there is a stepped approach to counter moves that progresses as follows:

1. "You are wrong," with volumes of reasons to support this.

2. "Change back and we will accept you again."

3. "If you don't change back, these are the consequences," which are then listed.

We [those making the changes] may be accused of coldness, disloyalty, selfishness, or disregard for others…We may receive verbal or nonverbal threats that the other person will withdraw or terminate the relationship… people do not make countermoves simply because they are dominating or controlling. They may or may not be these things, but that is almost beside the point. Countermoves are an expression of anxiety, as well as of closeness and attachment. Countermoves are the other person's unconscious attempt to restore a relationship to its prior balance or equilibrium, when anxiety about separateness and change gets too high.[21]

Absence of symptoms confused as a cure

One of the more common sources of slips and lapses for younger patients is feeling that an ability to approach food and feel connected with hunger is a sign of a complete cure. And let's face it: plenty of mature patients can fall into this trap, too!

There is no cure for an eating disorder. So why bother to get to remission in the first place if it's so easy to slip and then quickly slide into full-blown relapse? It's a practice and as such the real rewards are not in hitting a finish line; they are in getting to know all the ways in which an eating disorder has shaped you for good and bad. If we consider that an eating disorder stems from a sensitive threat identification system, then ensuring that this system gets honed for your benefit rather than detriment is what the practice of remission is all about (slips, lapses, relapses and all).

Gwyneth: Why do you persist with recovery efforts?

Patient N: I have seen a close family member struggle with an eating disorder for two decades, and continue to struggle long after she was declared "recovered" by her doctors. MM§ recovery promised a way beyond that fragile "recovery", and stripped away the mystery and the bizarre reverence anorexia sometimes attracts, and laid out clearly the path to a robust recovery. It made so much sense to me, and even when recovery got (really) tough, I knew on some level that eating enough and resting were the right things to do, and that there was something seriously wrong with society's attitudes towards food, body image, and weight.

Now I persist because I am experiencing true remission, and I never want to do anything to jeopardise that. I'm not making much of an effort these days, because eating and taking care of myself come pretty naturally – but at the back of my mind, there's a scrap of paper curled in a corner somewhere with the words "eat, rest, breathe" scrawled on it… I know I can retrieve if I need to.

---

§ Homeodynamic Recovery Method

End Notes for Chapter Seven

1. Barbara B. Kahn and Jeffrey S. Flier, "Obesity and insulin resistance," *The Journal of Clinical Investigation* 106, no. 4 (2000): 473-481.

2. Stacey S. Cofield, Rachel V. Corona, and David B. Allison, "Use of Causal Language in Observational Studies of Obesity and Nutrition," *Obesity Facts* 3, no. 6 (2010): 353-356.

3. Carl J. Lavie, Richard V. Milani, and Hector O. Ventura, "Obesity and Cardiovascular Disease: Risk Factor, Paradox, and Impact of Weight Loss," *Journal of the American College of Cardiology* 53, no. 21 (2009): 1925-1932.

4. Seth Uretsky, Franz H. Messerli, Sripal Bangalore, Annette Champion, Rhonda M. Cooper-DeHoff, Qian Zhou, and Carl J. Pepine, "Obesity paradox in patients with hypertension and coronary artery disease," *The American Journal of Medicine* 120, no. 10 (2007): 863-870.

5. John T. Mullen, Donald W. Moorman, and Daniel L. Davenport, "The obesity paradox: body mass index and outcomes in patients undergoing nonbariatric general surgery," *Annals of Surgery* 250, no. 1 (2009): 166-172.

6. Chin-Hsiao Tseng, "Obesity paradox: differential effects on cancer and noncancer mortality in patients with type 2 diabetes mellitus," *Atherosclerosis* 226, no. 1 (2013): 186-192.

7. Rexford S. Ahima, "Central actions of adipocyte hormones," *Trends in Endocrinology & Metabolism* 16, no. 7 (2005): 307-313.

8. Jeanine C. Cogan and Paul Ernsberger, "Dieting, Weight, and Health: Reconceptualizing Research and Policy," *Journal of Social Issues* 55, no. 2 (1999): 187-205.

9. Mary C. Tierney, Rahim Moineddin, Angela Morra, Judith Manson, and Jennifer Blake, "Intensity of Recreational Physical Activity throughout Life and Later Life Cognitive Functioning in Women," *Journal of Alzheimer's Disease* 22, no. 4 (2010): 1331-1338.

10. Erick Prado de Oliveira and Roberto Carlos Burini, "The impact of physical exercise on the gastrointestinal tract," *Current Opinion in Clinical Nutrition & Metabolic* Care 12, no. 5 (2009): 533-538.

11. I-Min Lee and Ralph S. Paffenbarger Jr., "Associations of Light, Moderate, and Vigorous Intensity Physical Activity with Longevity: The Harvard Alumni Health Study," *American Journal of Epidemiology* 151, no. 3 (2000): 293-299.

12. A. Inui, "Eating behavior in anorexia nervosa—an excess of both orexigenic and anorexigenic signalling?" *Molecular Psychiatry* 6, no. 6 (2001): 620-624.

13. Anton J. W. Scheurink, Gretha J. Boersma, Ricard Nergårdh, and Per Södersten, "Neurobiology of hyperactivity and reward: Agreeable restlessness in Anorexia Nervosa," *Physiology & Behavior* 100, no. 5 (2010): 490-495.

14. Serguei O. Fetissov, Maria Hamze Sinno, Quentin Coquerel, Jean Claude Do Rego, Moïse Coëffier, Danièle Gilbert, Tomas Hökfelt, and Pierre Déchelotte, "Emerging role of autoantibodies against appetite-regulating neuropeptides in eating disorders," *Nutrition* 24, no. 9 (2008): 854-859.

15. Cesar A. Hincapié and J. David Cassidy, "Disordered eating, menstrual disturbances, and low bone mineral density in dancers: a systematic review," *Archives of Physical Medicine and Rehabilitation* 91, no. 11 (2010): 1777-1789.e1.

16. Paolo Santonastaso, Silvia Mondini, and Angela Favaro, "Are Fashion Models a Group at Risk for Eating Disorders and Substance Abuse?" *Psychotherapy and Psychosomatics* 71, no. 3 (2002): 168-172.

17. Viren Swami and Emilia Szmigielska, "Body image concerns in professional fashion models: Are they really an at-risk group?" *Psychiatry Research* 207, 1-2 (2013): 113-117.

18. Jorunn Sundgot-Borgen and Monica Klungland Torstveit, "Prevalence of Eating Disorders in Elite Athletes Is Higher Than in the General Population," *Clinical Journal of Sport Medicine* 14, no. 1 (2004): 25-32.

19. Gabriela Morgado de Oliveira Coelho, Eliane de Abreu Soares, and Beatriz Gonçalves Ribeiro, "Are female athletes at increased risk for disordered eating and its complications?" *Appetite* 55, no. 3 (2010): 379-387.

20. Mary Ann Crossno, "Bowen Family Systems Theory," in *Marriage and Family Therapy: A Practice-Oriented Approach*, ed. Linda Metcalf and (New York: Springer Publishing Company, 2011), 39-64.

21. Harriet Lerner, "Trying out a "New You"? Prepare for Counter-moves!" *Psychology Today: The Dance of Connection* (blog), December 22, 2013, https://www.psychologytoday.com/blog/the-dance-connection/201312/trying-out-new-you-prepare-countermoves.

ABOUT THE AUTHOR

Gwyneth Olwyn is a patient advocate, member of the Alliance of Professional Health Advocates, and founder of the Eating Disorder Institute.

Not having an eating disorder herself, Gwyneth's interest in the area of eating disorders came about from her years spent researching recovery options for patients with the condition. The Eating Disorder Institute is the result of this ongoing intensive research and synthesis (since 2009) on the topic of science-based options for recovery from an eating disorder.

Gwyneth lives and works in Vancouver Canada.

Made in the USA
San Bernardino, CA
27 December 2018